# DINING IN-SAN FRANCISCO

Especially for:

*Mar + Frank*

with our compliments
for your dining pleasure
from your friends at

**southern california savings**

SOUTHERN CALIFORNIA
SAVINGS AND LOAN ASSOCIATION
645 TAMALPAIS DRIVE
CORTE MADERA, CA 94925

## TITLES IN SERIES:

# DINING IN-SAN FRANCISCO

By Rona Abbott and Jane Olsen

PEANUT BUTTER PUBLISHING

Peanut Butter Towers     Seattle, Washington 98134

First Printing March, 1978
Second Printing September, 1978
Third Printing September, 1979
Fourth Printing March, 1981

ISBN 0-89716-017-7

# CONTENTS

# INTRODUCTION

After I received a call from Peanut Butter Publishing asking me to write an introduction to DINING IN—SAN FRANCISCO, I became jubilant. You see, this is precisely the kind of book I have always dreamed about. Being a native San Franciscan I have dined in literally hundreds of this City's restaurants, and over the years I have become convinced that no other city has a greater group of restaurants than San Francisco. The many, many choices available are overwhelming!

Let me qualify my upcoming remarks by stating here that I love San Francisco: its climate, its cosmopolitan nature, its people and especially its cuisine. First a few facts before I continue this commentary. At last count there were over 1500 different restaurants in the City! We have more eating establishments per resident than any other city in the United States. In a boundary of 44 square miles you could eat in a different restaurant every day for more than four years and by the time you had finished, you'd have to start over again to try all the new places that had opened in the interim. Almost daily a new restaurant is opening somewhere in the City.

Not only is this City abundant in restaurants, but it offers an amazing diversity for their patrons. There are traditional ones, with at least ten over one hundred years old, as well as some of the most avant garde restaurants in America. When it comes to ethnic cooking I don't think any city has a greater group. Even the yellow pages list our restaurants by nationality, alphabetically from Alsatian to Vietnamese.

There are certain styles of cuisine that are most exceptional and unique to San Francisco. Any discussion of this sort must begin by mentioning the fabulous seafood found in our City, especially down at Fisherman's Wharf. I, for one, have never been able to resist the smells found there of freshly caught crab, clams, abalone, sand dabs, salmon and the like.

Our restaurants also take advantage of the wonderful climate. The weather in Northern California is perfect for the production of two of our gastronomic delights—wine and sourdough bread. These are certainly two of our natural resources. With the Napa Valley at our back door, San Francisco restaurants have a huge assortment of fine California wines in addition to the imported wines. Another treat unique to San Francisco is our sourdough bread which can only be made here because of the climate. In my travels, I have found no other city that sells bread by the loaf in the airport.

We all enjoy the excitement, ambiance and luxury of dining out. But DINING IN adds the unique satisfaction provided when a fine meal is prepared by one's own hands. When we serve a meal to our friends and loved ones we gain the greatest sense of joy—the gift of giving. The revival of interest in gourmet cooking taking place in homes throughout the country points to the personal satisfaction that cooking can offer.

At least I wasn't assigned the task of choosing the twenty-one restaurants included here. It certainly must have been a tough choice. Another difficult task must have been experienced by the restaurants themselves — selecting only one meal from all their specialties could not have been easy. This book most assuredly contains the crème de la crème!

Thus, this book serves a dual purpose — offering restaurant recommendations along with their finest recipes. Whether you decide to eat in or out, once you have DINING IN—SAN FRANCISCO, all you need is a healthy appetite. Have fun and bon appétit.

Cyril Magnin

*Dinner for Four*

*Vol-au-Vent of Crab Legs and Lobster Amoricaine*

*Caesar Salad*

*Veal Scaloppine à la Doros with Parisienne Potatoes*

*Braised Belgian Endive*

*Grand Marnier Soufflé with Zabaglione Sauce*

*Coffee*

*Courvoisier*

*Wine:*

*With Crab Legs and Lobster—*
*Mondavi Fumé Blanc, 1976*

*With Veal—Mondavi Chardonnay, 1973*

*With Soufflé—Almadén Vineyards Johannisberg*
*Riesling, Late Harvest, 1975*

*Don Dianda, Owner*

*Paolo Bermani, Executive Chef*

Don Dianda opened Doros on Montgomery Street twenty years ago. He says, "We call our menu 'continental cuisine' but in truth it is 'world cuisine'. Our food is prepared in the classical manner with sauces, herbs and garniture.

"We try to give the customer a total experience in dining. To do so takes a courteous, well-run organization, a good staff in the kitchen as well as in the dining room, and good ambiance. Dining out should be an adventure, the customer is king or queen for the night.

"People's likes and dislikes change continually and we try to provide for that. Our menus are revised periodically. A change of foods is not only rewarding but it is healthy for the body.

"We have a cross-section of guests from all over the world and we have become more international without trying. It is the people themselves who have created the restaurant. This is my home away from home and who's luckier than I!"

Chef Bermani, a native of San Remo, came to this country in 1939 and has been involved in the preparation of food ever since.

"If a guest comes in and asks for a dish which is not on our menu, we'll make it for him," he says. "The hardest thing I've ever had to cook is wild boar."

The restaurant has received consecutive Holiday Magazine Awards since 1961 and the Mobil Travel Guide Four-Star Award for 1977.

## VOL-AU-VENT OF CRAB LEGS AND LOBSTER AMORICAINE

***Some people call this sauce 'Americaine' but it is really Amoricaine and comes from northern France.  If you cannot find fresh lobster, I suggest that you buy frozen Australian lobster tail.***

1 lb. lobster, fresh (or frozen tail)
16 crab legs, boiled
4 vol-au-vents (patty shells)
1 cup peeled tomatoes
2/3 cup cognac
1/4 cup sherry
5 oz. butter
1/2 cup heavy cream
1 T. Parmesan cheese, grated
Tabasco sauce
Salt

1.  Cut lobster in half, lengthwise.  Remove and discard intestinal vein.
2.  Melt 4 oz. of the butter in a skillet.  Add lobster (in shell), and sear until it becomes red, turning it a few times with tongs.
3.  Flambé with 1/3 cup cognac.
4.  When flames die, add 1/4 cup sherry and cook for 3 minutes.
5.  Add tomatoes and season with salt and a dash of Tabasco sauce. Continue cooking for about 10 minutes.
6.  Remove lobster from shell and dice.
7.  Meanwhile, in another skillet, melt 1 oz. of the butter until golden brown and add the freshly cooked crab legs.  Flambé with the remaining cognac.
8.  Add diced lobster meat.
9.  Strain the lobster sauce and add heavy cream.  Stir until smooth.
10.  Add 2 T. of the sauce to the lobster and crab legs mixture, mixing thoroughly.
11.  Fill the patty shells with the mixture and set on a platter.
12.  Pour the remaining sauce over the shells and sprinkle with cheese. Place under the broiler for 1 minute and serve immediately.

## CAESAR SALAD

***Remember to use cold salad plates.***

3 anchovies
1/8 t. powdered dry mustard
1/4 t. horseradish
1 t. fresh lemon juice
1 T. red wine vinegar
3 T. olive oil
2 cups dry, crisp romaine lettuce, in 1 inch pieces
1 cup dry, crisp iceberg lettuce, in 1 inch pieces
1/4 t. salt
Freshly ground pepper
1/2 cup dry, crisp croutons
2 T. garlic-flavored oil
3 to 4 T. Parmesan cheese
1 coddled egg

1. Place anchovies on a small plate. Sprinkle mustard, horseradish, lemon juice, vinegar and olive oil on top. Mash ingredients into a smooth paste with a fork.
2. Put the salad greens into a large salad bowl set in ice. Sprinkle with salt and a good covering of freshly ground pepper.
3. Toss croutons with garlic-flavored oil.
4. Add the anchovy paste and croutons. Sprinkle the cheese over the top.
5. Put the coddled egg on top and toss until the leaves are coated. Serve immediately.

***When cooking, first prepare yourself mentally for what you want to achieve. Try to do what you know best — plain, light foods — and slowly work on improving as you go along. If you stay in a happy frame of mind and cook the food with the right amount of seasoning, and serve it beautifully, then the meal will be a success.***

## VEAL SCALOPPINE À LA DOROS

***The preparation of this dish is the most important part since the actual cooking does not take very long. You may want to purchase the brown sauce instead of fixing it at home.***

12 thin slices veal loin, pounded flat
Salt
Pepper
Flour
1 cup plus 2 T. butter
1/4 cup dry sauterne
1 lb. mushrooms, sliced
1/2 cup brown sauce
12 slices eggplant
1 T. shallots or green onions, finely chopped
Chopped fresh parsley
Parisienne Potatoes

1. Season veal with salt and pepper. Dip in flour to lightly cover both sides.
2. Melt 1 cup of the butter in a large skillet. When it bubbles, add the veal slices and brown on both sides.
3. Pour off excess butter and add the shallots. Pour in the wine and simmer for 3 minutes.
4. Add brown sauce.
5. In a separate pan, sauté the mushrooms.
6. In a separate pan, sauté the eggplant.
7. Arrange veal and eggplant alternately on a bed of sautéed mushrooms.
8. To the rest of the sauce in the skillet add 2 T. solid butter. Shake the skillet to swirl and melt the butter. Pour the sauce over the veal and eggplant slices and serve immediately with Parisienne Potatoes and Braised Belgian Endive.

***You don't need a big or fancy kitchen to cook well. All you need is heart and soul.***

### BRAISED BELGIAN ENDIVE

2 heads Belgian endive (about 3/4 lb. total)
2 cups beef stock
1 T. butter
2 T. rich veal stock
Salt
Pepper

1. Halve endive and boil in beef stock. Season with salt and pepper to taste.
2. During the last 5 minutes of cooking, drain the beef stock and add butter and veal stock. Braise until evenly coated.
3. Set endive on a platter and top with sauce to serve.

### GRAND MARNIER SOUFFLÉ

***The secret of preparing a good soufflé is to make certain that you have allowed your ingredients to cool sufficiently *before* you add the egg whites. Otherwise, the whites will lose some of their volume. It is best to prepare the recipe just before baking. Should you go wrong, don't feel too bad. Even the professionals sometimes have problems.***

3/4 cup milk
2 T. sugar
1 t. vanilla
3 T. sifted flour
Cold milk
3 egg yolks
2 T. butter
2 T. Grand Marnier
4 egg whites
Sprinkle of powdered sugar

1. Boil 3/4 cup milk with sugar.
2. Add vanilla and sifted flour which has been diluted in a tiny bit of cold milk. Cook, stirring constantly, for about 4 minutes. Remove from heat.
3. Add egg yolks, butter and Grand Marnier. Cool for a few minutes.
4. Add stiffly beaten egg whites.
5. Butter and sugar 4 individual soufflé dishes. (One large serving dish may be used.)
6. Fill dishes with batter and set in a pan of hot water. Bake at 450° for about 20 minutes.
7. Remove from oven and sprinkle with powdered sugar to decorate top. Serve with Zabaglione Sauce.


## ZABAGLIONE SAUCE

***Don't worry about preparing this sauce. It is not as tricky as regular zabaglione because this is a thinner consistency.***

5 egg yolks
4 oz. sauterne
4 oz. Marsala
2 heaping T. sugar
2 oz. Grand Marnier

1. Place egg yolks, sauterne, Marsala and sugar in top of a double boiler. Whip over boiling water until very fluffy.
2. Remove from heat and blend in Grand Marnier. Serve with soufflé.

NOTE: "For a wonderful sauce to serve with strawberries, add heavy cream and chill."

*Dinner for Four*

*Little Snails in Clay Pots*

*Cream of Artichoke Soup with Hazelnuts*

*Roast Native Duckling with Green Peppercorn
and Kumquat Sauce*

*String Beans*

*Butter Lettuce Ravigote Salad*

*Dacquoise*

*Wine:*

*With Snails and Soup—Chappellet Chenin Blanc,
Napa Valley, 1975*

*With Duckling—Joseph Phelps Cabernet Sauvignon,
St. Helena, 1973*

*With Dacquoise—Schramsberg Blanc de Noir,
Napa Valley*

*James A. Nassikas, President*

*Marcel Dragon, Chef de Cuisine*

Fournou's Ovens derives its name from the word for oven in several Romance languages. The restaurant is designed around the huge ovens, faced in French provincial tile, where guests can see lamb, duck or beef roasted.

Antiques collected from five countries decorate the walls and dining terraces. Terra cotta tile floors, weathered wood, antique brass fixtures and whitewashed walls set the mood for fine dining.

The restaurant is located in the elegant Stanford Court Hotel on Nob Hill. But Fournou's is not a typical hotel dining room. It has drawn superlative reviews, the Holiday Magazine Fine Dining Award and the Mainliner United Airlines Dining Award.

Chef de cuisine Marcel Dragon began his career thirty-eight years ago at the Hotel de Paris in Monte Carlo where he prepared menus and tables for such international luminaries as the Aga Khan and Sir Winston Churchill. He later served as chef saucier at the Crillon in Paris, the Colony in New York and as chef at Le Manoir in Chicago. He joined Fournou's Ovens five years ago.

## LITTLE SNAILS IN CLAY POTS

***I love to eat snails—one of my very favorite dishes! These snails are prepared in tiny clay pots which are imported from France and which can be found in most gourmet specialty shops.***

6 hazelnuts, peeled and finely chopped
6 oz. butter, unsalted
3/4 oz. shallots, finely chopped
2 garlic cloves, crushed
1 T. parsley, finely chopped
24 shell snails
Rock salt
Metal escargot dishes for cooking
Clay pots

1. Mix butter, shallots, garlic, parsley and nuts. Whip to a cream.
2. Place each snail in its own clay pot. Cover the snail with a generous amount of the butter mixture.
3. Fill each metal dish with white rock salt and arrange the clay pots by partially immersing them in the salt.
4. Bake in a 375° oven for about 12 minutes, until done.

NOTE: Snail pots can be covered with a cap of puff paste and baked until golden brown.

## CREAM OF ARTICHOKE SOUP WITH HAZELNUTS

1/2 lb. large artichokes, whole
1 oz. hazelnuts
1/2 cup heavy cream
1 qt. chicken stock
2 oz. rice flour
1/2 oz. sherry
Salt
Pepper

1. Remove all leaves and stems from fresh, large artichokes. Clean and scoop artichokes, using bottoms or pedestals only.
2. Poach artichoke bottoms in water for 1 hour. Remove from water and place in chicken stock.
3. Roast hazelnuts in a 250° oven until golden brown (about 10 minutes).
4. Crush nuts to a fine consistency.
5. Add nuts to the chicken stock and artichoke bottoms and simmer mixture for 1/2 hour.
6. Pass all the ingredients through a sieve.
7. Thicken with rice flour and simmer for 1/4 hour.
8. Add salt, pepper and cream. Finish with sherry to taste.

## ROAST NATIVE DUCKLING WITH GREEN PEPPERCORN AND KUMQUAT SAUCE

***A good duck should be about four to five pounds. When you buy one be sure to test for tenderness by bending the point of the breast which is away from the wing. If it doesn't bend, the bird will be tough. This test also works for chicken. Of course, freshness is very important. The duck which is served here is dressed in Petaluma at 3 am. It arrives in Chinatown at 9 am and in our kitchen by 10 or 11 am. All Americans do not like duck but at Fournou's we serve even more than I did in Europe.***

2 ducks, 4 to 5 pounds each, dressed
1/2 large onion, coarsely chopped
1/2 stalk celery, cut in 1 inch slices
2 carrots, peeled and sliced
6 fresh kumquats
2 t. vinegar
1 oz. sugar, granulated
2 cups fresh orange juice
Juice of 2 lemons
2 t. black peppercorns, crushed
1 bay leaf
1 small sprig thyme
1 small leek, sliced finely
1/2 pt. demi-glace or gravy (canned may be used)
1/2 cup tomato paste
1 oz. jigger Cointreau or Grand Marnier
3 oz. green peppercorns, whole
Salt
Pepper

1. Wipe and dry ducks. Fill each duck cavity with one half the amount of celery, onion and carrots. Sprinkle with salt and pepper.
2. Roast ducks at 425° for 45 minutes on a rack to allow fat to drain.
3. Peel half of the kumquats, removing all pulp from peel.
4. Cut peels in fine julienne. Cover with boiling water for 1 minute. Drain and reserve.
5. In a saucepan, cook vinegar and sugar over medium heat until mixture begins to caramelize.
6. Add orange and lemon juice and the pulp from the peeled kumquats. Cook until liquid reduces about one-fourth.
7. Add the kumquat julienne, crushed peppercorns, bay leaf, thyme and leek. Simmer until golden brown.
8. Add the gravy and tomato paste. Simmer, stirring occasionally, for 1 hour.
9. Strain through a fine sieve and add the liqueur and whole green peppercorns.
10. Drain all juices and fat from roasted ducks. Halve them and arrange on heated platters.
11. Garnish with remaining kumquats cut in thin slices. Reheat sauce and serve separately.

STRING BEANS

***At Fournou's Ovens our vegetables change daily.  Our food must be absolutely fresh—not frozen.  Frozen food is never as good and there is always the loss of vitamins.  The European method of daily shopping is still the best for the cook at home.***

8 oz. fresh string beans
1 oz. butter
Salt
White pepper

1.  Wash and prepare beans.
2.  Boil until just tender crisp.
3.  Heat butter in a skillet.  Sauté the beans with a bit of salt and white pepper and serve.

***To be a good cook you must have a willingness to learn.  The preparation of a good meal takes a lot of time and work.***

## BUTTER LETTUCE RAVIGOTE SALAD

2 heads butter lettuce
2 oz. oil
2 oz. vinegar
4 shallots, chopped
2 t. capers, chopped
1 bunch fresh tarragon, chopped
Salt (pinch)
White pepper (pinch)

1. Wash lettuce. Split in half and remove core. Arrange on plates.
2. Combine all remaining ingredients and pour over lettuce.

***I have worked in New York, Philadelphia and Chicago but San Francisco is the top. It is truly the country's number one city of fine restaurants.***

### DACQUOISE

***This is a very beautiful dessert brought to us by James Beard.
We serve it each night.***

### MERINGUE

6 egg whites
12 T. sugar
3/4 cup ground walnuts and hazelnuts
1 T. cornstarch
1/8 t. cream of tartar
1 t. vanilla extract
1/8 t. almond extract

1. Beat the egg whites until they are foamy. Add salt and cream of tartar. Continue beating until you have soft peaks.
2. Slowly add 10 T. of the sugar and beat to stiff peaks. Beat in the vanilla and almond extracts.
3. Combine the nut mixture, cornstarch and the last 2 T. of sugar. Mix thoroughly. Fold gently into the meringue.
4. Draw two 10 inch circles on parchment paper and place on baking sheets.
5. Scoop meringue mixture into a pastry bag with a 3/8 inch tip. Fill circles with the meringue and bake in the middle upper level of a 200° oven until firm. Meringue should be dry but not brown.
6. Cool to room temperature and use a wide spatula to remove the rounds to a wire rack to cool.

## MOCHA BUTTER CREAM

3/4 cup milk
3 egg yolks
1¼ cups confectioners' sugar
3 oz. butter (soft)
3 T. instant coffee
1 T. hot water
2 T. cognac

1. Heat milk to the boiling point.
2. Meanwhile, combine yolks and confectioners' sugar in the bowl of an electric mixer and blend. When the milk begins to boil pour it into the yolk-sugar mixture and blend thoroughly.
3. Pour the custard back into a saucepan and return to heat. Beat until well thickened, stirring more or less continuously.
4. Pour back into the bowl of the electric mixer and beat at high speed until cool.
5. Add soft butter in small pieces. When butter is completely absorbed, beat at high speed until fluffy.
6. Add 3 T. instant coffee which has been dissolved in hot water and the cognac, if desired.

## TO ASSEMBLE:

1. Place one round of the baked meringue on a cake platter. With a spatula, spread 2/3 of the mocha cream over the meringue to within 1/2 inch of the edge.
2. Put remaining cream into pastry bag with a star tip and create a decorative border around the edge of the meringue.
3. Gently place the second meringue on top. Sprinkle with confectioners' sugar and serve at once or refrigerate.

NOTE: Do not refrigerate more than 2 hours or the meringue will soften.

*Dinner for Four*

*Diced Winter Melon Soup*

*Sai Wo Duck*

*Button Mushrooms and Lobster*

*Gourmet Vegetables*

*Oyster Beef*

*Yeong Jo Fried Rice*

*Fortune Cookies*

*Wine:*

*Wan Fu White Wine*

*Guy Wong, Owner and Manager*

*Sun Pui Wong, Executive Chef*

To many San Franciscans, the late Johnny Kan epitomized "Mr. Chinatown". Associated with supplying food in one way or another since boyhood, he learned Chinese cooking from his mother, who operated a small restaurant in the rear of his father's store. He later opened his famous restaurant on Grant Street "dedicated to all that is genuine and worthwhile in Chinese cuisine".

Manager-owner Guy Wong, a long-time friend of Kan, continues this policy. Wong says, "We take great care in the preparation of the dishes. Our kitchen is capable of making anything. We use very fresh foods that are in season."

This care, service, and decor are responsible for the many awards which the restaurant has received. Since 1957, Kan's has won consecutive Holiday Magazine Awards. It is also a Mobil Travel Guide Four-Star Award winner.

During his long career, Kan introduced many 'firsts', including the Chinese Kitchen, the first delivery service for Chinese food. The idea and the name are now widely used all over the United States.

Lots of celebrities frequent Kan's. It was here that Danny Kaye developed his interest in Chinese cuisine and his desire to become a qualified Chinese chef. Wong adds, "He's a very devoted person. When he wanted to learn to bone a chicken, he was in the kitchen practicing for hours."

Chef Sun Pui Wong, a cook for sixteen years, has been regularly selected to participate in the 'Master Chefs on Parade' programs of the Western National Convention and Educational Exposition.

The following recipes are from Johnny Kan's "Eight Immortal Flavors".

## DICED WINTER MELON SOUP

5 cups soup stock or chicken broth
1/2 lb. winter melon, diced
1/4 cup chicken, diced
4 water chestnuts, diced
Salt
MSG

1. Place stock or broth in a pot. Cover and bring to a boil.
2. Add winter melon, chicken and water chestnuts.
3. Simmer 10 minutes. Season to taste with salt and MSG.

## SAI WO DUCK

***This dish will require a good deal of time for preparation but if you follow the recipe everything will turn out well.***

1 duckling, medium-sized, dressed
Soy sauce (to rub over duckling)
2 stalks celery
1 whole green onion
4 thin slices ginger root
5 Chinese black mushrooms, presoaked
2 pieces dried Mandarin orange peel (size of a half dollar), presoaked
5 thinly sliced pieces bamboo shoots
10 star anise seeds
1¼ t. salt
1/4 t. sugar
Pepper (dash)
1 t. MSG (optional)
1 T. cornstarch
1 T. soy sauce
Chinese parsley
Vegetable oil for frying
Loose lettuce leaves (garnish)

1. Rub soy sauce over duckling.
2. Using a large deep-fry pan boil enough oil to cover the bird. Add duckling and fry until the entire bird is well-browned. Remove and drain on absorbent toweling.
3. Use a sharp cleaver to slash the duck, starting from the breast down to the lower belly. *Do not cut through bone.*
4. Place duck in a pan and stuff the cavity with the celery, onion, ginger root, black mushrooms, orange peel, bamboo shoots, anise, 1 t. salt, sugar, pepper, and MSG (if desired). Distribute evenly.
5. Place duck on a platter and elevate it in a steamer. Cover and steam for 2½ hours. Make sure that the water is replenished as it evaporates.
6. Remove platter and allow duck to cool. Discard all ingredients except bamboo shoots and mushrooms. Save all the juices for gravy.
7. Carefully remove wings and legs. Using hands, gently separate the flesh from the carcass, starting from the slash and keeping the skin intact. Be sure not to make any more holes in the skin and to keep the bird in its natural shape. (Carcass will make good soup.)
8. Spread duck, meat side up, on a deep platter. De-bone the legs and place with wings.
9. Spread the mushrooms and bamboo shoots over the duck meat.
10. Replace in steaming utensil and steam again for 20 minutes. Remove.
11. Line a large serving platter with lettuce leaves. Turn the platter with the duck upside-down so that the duck rests on the leaves, skin side up.
12. Pour the cooking juices into a saucepan. There should be about 2 cups liquid. Bring to a boil, over high heat.
13. Add cornstarch, 1 T. soy sauce and 1/4 t. salt. Stir continuously until the gravy thickens.
14. Pour the gravy over the whole duck. Garnish with Chinese parsley and serve immediately.

***We recommend that you use chopsticks. Remember that they can be a great diet tool—if you can't pick up the food you can't eat it.***

## BUTTON MUSHROOMS AND LOBSTER

Meat from 2 lobster tails, sliced into 1/2 inch pieces
1 small can button mushrooms, drained
1/2 cup canned bamboo shoots, sliced about 1/4 inch thick and into
    3/4 inch pieces
1/2 cup celery, thinly sliced
2 T. vegetable oil
1/2 t. salt
1/3 t. sugar
1 t. soy sauce

1/2 t. MSG (optional)
1 cup chicken stock
1 T. cornstarch made into a paste with 1 T. water

1.  Add oil and salt to preheated skillet or wok.  Bring oil to sizzling
point over high heat.
2.  Add lobster meat.  Toss and turn rapidly for 2 minutes.
3.  Add the vegetables, sugar, soy sauce, chicken stock and MSG (if
desired).  Turn ingredients lightly until thoroughly mixed.  Cover and
cook over high heat for 7 minutes.
4.  Uncover and gradually add the cornstarch/water paste.  Cook until sauce has thickened.  Serve.


## GOURMET VEGETABLES

1/2 cup raw beef, finely sliced
1½ cups bamboo shoots, finely sliced
1/2 cup Chinese dried mushrooms (presoaked), finely sliced
1 cup celery, finely sliced
1/3 cup sliced dried onion, finely sliced
1½ cups rice sticks (Mai Fun)
2 T. vegetable oil plus oil for deep frying
1 t. salt
1/2 cup chicken stock
1/2 t. MSG (optional)
1 t. soy sauce
1/2 t. sugar
2 t. cornstarch made into a paste with 2 t. water

1.  In a deep-fat fryer, heat oil to 350°. Add rice sticks and cook until light and crisp.
2.  Put 2 T. vegetable oil into a preheated wok or skillet and using a high heat bring oil to a sizzle.
3.  Add beef and toss and turn rapidly for 1 to 2 minutes. Remove from pan when half-cooked.
4.  Into the same utensil add the salt and all the sliced ingredients. Bring to a medium-high heat and toss and turn all ingredients for about 2 minutes.
5.  Add chicken stock combined with MSG (if desired). Cover and cook over medium heat for 3 minutes.
6.  Add soy sauce, sugar and the half-cooked beef.
7.  Increase to a high heat and continue to toss-cook.
8.  When all ingredients are thoroughly blended, immediately add cornstarch/water paste. Toss-cook just until sauce thickens, about 1 minute, no longer. Place on serving dish and top with crisp rice sticks.

OYSTER BEEF

***Oyster Sauce in Chinese translates as Ho Yow.***

1 lb. beef, sliced 1/4 inch thick (2 X 1 inch pieces)
1/2 cup scallions, white sections only, cut into 1 inch lengths
1/4 t. salt
1/2 t. soy sauce
1 t. cornstarch
Sugar (dash)
2 T. vegetable oil
2 T. oyster sauce
1/4 cup chicken stock
1/4 t. MSG (optional)
1 T. cornstarch made into a paste with 1 T. water

1.  In a mixing bowl, combine salt, soy sauce, 1 t. cornstarch and sugar. Blend thoroughly and add sliced beef. Marinate 5 minutes.
2.  Add oil to a preheated wok or skillet. Add beef, scallions, and oyster sauce. Toss-cook at high heat for 3 minutes.
3.  Add chicken stock, MSG (if desired), and cornstarch/water paste. Mix and toss until gravy thickens and has coated the beef and scallions. Serve very hot.

## YEONG JO FRIED RICE

1/4 cup raw prawns or shrimp, diced
1/4 cup barbecued pork or cooked ham, diced
1/4 cup green onions, cut 1/8 inch thick
1/4 cup green peas
1 cup lettuce, shredded
3 cups cold cooked rice
2 T. vegetable oil
1/2 t. salt
2 T. soy sauce

1. Place oil in a preheated wok or skillet. Bring oil to sizzling point and add prawns or shrimp and salt.
2. Toss and turn for 2 to 3 minutes or until cooked.
3. Add pork or ham, green onions, peas, lettuce, rice and soy sauce. Press rice gently into the pan and fry for a few seconds, repeating the process until all the rice is hot completely through. Turn and mix rapidly for 5 to 7 minutes. Add a few drops of oil if necessary to prevent burning.

***White rice may be substituted for Yeong Jo Fried Rice.***

***The secret of cooking Chinese food is being able to time correctly the preparation of each dish. Preparation is the essential part of our cuisine, and requires practice. Cooking takes only a few minutes.***

***Chinese food differs from Western cuisine in that our meats and vegetables are cut into bite-sized pieces *before* they are served.***

*Dinner for Six*

*Avocado à la Horcher's*

*Tortellini*

*Tournedo de Boeuf Rossini*

*Mousse Tia Maria*

*Wine:*

*California Cabernet Sauvignon*

*Victor and Roland Gotti, Owners*
*Jacky Robert, Head Chef*

Ernie's is located on the edge of what was once the infamous Barbary Coast. It originally opened as a dance hall featuring the long bar which was carried around the Horn in a sailing ship. Later the dance hall became a family style restaurant, Ernie's II Travatore. In 1935 Ambrogio Gotti joined Ernie Carlesso in the business and changed the name to Ernie's. Gotti's sons Victor and Roland later renovated the building and transformed the restaurant into its present Victorian decor.

Ernie's has become a city landmark and a popular location for films and television. Lucius Beebe dined here regularly and served as the Gotti brothers' "unofficial" counsel in building their extensive wine list. The restaurant has received the Holiday Magazine Dining Award for twenty-three consecutive years and the Mobil Travel Guide Five-Star Award for fifteen years.

Head chef Jacky Robert was born in Normandy, France and studied cooking in France, primarily at Maxim's.

## AVOCADO À LA HORCHER'S

***This dish honors Otto Horcher, a famous Madrid restaurateur.***

1½ lbs. frozen imported scampi (already cooked)
3 avocados
Cocktail sauce

1. Thaw scampi in the refrigerator for 24 hours or overnight.
2. Mix scampi with cocktail sauce.
3. Make small balls of avocado with a melon baller.
4. Into individual cocktail dishes place a layer of avocado balls, a layer of scampi and a topping of sauce. Serve chilled.

## TORTELLINI

72 tortellini
1 cup Parmesan cheese, grated
2 T. butter
1½ cups half & half
2 egg yolks
Salt
Pepper
Water for cooking

1. Cook tortellini in boiling salted water for 10 minutes. Drain.
2. Place in a shallow pan and add half & half and butter. Heat but do not boil.
3. Add grated cheese and stir until thickened.
4. Remove from heat and season with a touch of salt and pepper. Add egg yolks. Mix well and serve.

## TOURNEDO DE BOEUF ROSSINI

36 oz. center of filet, cleaned
6 mushroom heads
1 to 2 truffles
6 oz. pâté de foie gras
Flour
1½ cups Madeira
1½ cups brown sauce
6 croutons—size of the tournedo
Salt
Pepper
Butter
Lard

1.  Insert a small piece of lard inside the filet.  Cut meat into 6 equal pieces.  Place sliced lard around each piece and tie to secure.
2.  Salt and pepper the top part of the filet.  Dredge the tops and bottoms with flour, excluding the lard-rimmed edge.
3.  Sauté over moderate heat.  Remove from pan and take off the sliced lard.  Remove fat.
4.  De-glaze with Madeira and chopped truffles.  (Set aside 6 slices of the truffle for later use.)  Add brown sauce.
5. To serve, place crouton on each plate and cover with tournedo. Top with 1 oz. pâté de foie gras, 1 truffle slice and 1 mushroom.  Add just enough sauce to cover.  Serve with remaining sauce on the side.

## MOUSSE TIA MARIA

2 cups milk
4 T. granulated sugar
1 T. all-purpose flour
1 T. gelatin
4 T. instant coffee
4 eggs
1 vanilla bean or 3 drops vanilla extract
Salt (pinch)
2 cups whipped cream
2 oz. Tia Maria liqueur
Cookies

1.  In a bowl, mix together eggs, vanilla, sugar, gelatin, coffee and salt.
Blend until the mixture heavily coats a spoon.
2.  Add flour and mix well, again.
3.  Boil milk and immediately pour it over the mixture, stirring gently
and continuously with a whip.
4.  Put mixture into a saucepan and bring to a boil, stirring constantly.
Remove from heat immediately and pour into a cold bowl.  Let cool.
5.  When completely cold, stir in whipped cream and Tia Maria and
pour into a glass dish.  Store in the refrigerator for at least 1 hour.
Serve with cookies.

FINE GERMAN FOOD
SINCE 1893

Schroeder's

*Dinner for Six*

*Schroeder's Sauerbraten*

*Potato Pancakes*

*Red Cabbage German Style*

*Soft Dessert Cheese with Apples or Winter Pears*

*Serve with Cabernet Sauvignon or German Beer*

*Max Sr., Max Jr. and Max III, Owners*

Schroeder's opened its doors in 1893. After being destroyed by the earthquake and fire, it was rebuilt on Front Street. For years, sea captains, merchants, businessmen and others enjoyed the 'men only' policy for lunch; not until 1970 was the restriction of not serving women before 1:30 pm finally withdrawn. "The young people like the girls around," says Max Jr.

Max Sr., now in his nineties, had been in the San Francisco restaurant business as a young man, returning to Germany during Prohibition. There he read in a Sunday issue of the "San Francisco Chronicle" that Mr. Schroeder had died. He knew the restaurant's reputation but had never set foot inside the door. In 1922 he returned to San Francisco and bought the business, sight unseen, from Schroeder's widow. The dishes listed on the current menu are his original recipes.

"I started just about when I got out of diapers," says Max Jr. "Our philosophy is to serve our customers fresh food each day. We have a relatively small menu of fourteen or fifteen items, but each one is prepared and used up daily."

Max III is manager. All three generations of Maxes drive to work together each morning.

## SCHROEDER'S SAUERBRATEN

***This is one of our specialties.  Max Sr. developed the recipe fifty-six years ago.***

5 lbs. beef, rump or top round, in one piece
2 cups vinegar
4 cups water
1 large onion, sliced
1/4 cup whole mixed spices for pickling
Salt to taste
2 T. sugar
3 T. flour
2 T. shortening
1/2 glass red wine

1.  Make a pickling solution of the vinegar, water, onions, spices, and a little salt.  Soak the meat in it for 2 to 3 days, turning frequently.
2.  Remove the meat from the liquid and place in hot fat.  Brown on all sides.  Remove to a tray or plate.
3.  Brown flour in the fat.  Add spices from the pickling solution, a little water, and sugar, and simmer for a few minutes.
4.  Place the browned meat in a roasting pan.  Add the sauce, cover and bake for 2½ to 3 hours in a 350  oven.  Turn and baste frequently.
5.  One half hour before meat is done, add the red wine.
6.  When done, lift meat to a hot platter.  Add water and flour paste to make a gravy and strain it into a gravy boat.  If sauce is not sour enough, add a little more vinegar.  Serve.

## POTATO PANCAKES

***These are easy to prepare.  Make sure the pancakes are brown and crisp.  Do not cover them before serving.***

3 lbs. raw potatoes
4 eggs
1¼ cups flour
1/2 T. salt
Pepper
1/2 t. grated onion
1 large sour apple, peeled and grated
Lard for frying

1.  Peel potatoes, wash and let stand in water.
2.  Remove from water and grate quickly.  Let drain.
3.  Add eggs, flour, pepper, salt, grated apple, and onion.
4.  Heat lard to a very hot temperature and cook 3 to 4 thin pancakes at a time.  Serve.

***Always make sure that your gravies are cooked long enough.  That way they will always be properly digested.  At Schroeder's we have a regular schedule for our sauces.  The first day, we roast the bones.  On the second day, the bones are put in a stock pot for brown sauce, and on the third, that particular brown stock is used for the final sauce.***

## RED CABBAGE GERMAN STYLE

***It is possible to prepare this dish one day ahead.  If you do, be sure to add an additional tablespoon or two of vinegar and one-quarter glass of red cooking wine to freshen the food just before serving.***

1 red cabbage, 4 lbs.
2 cups boiling broth
4 T. butter
2 T. vinegar
2 apples, peeled and cut
2 whole cloves
1/2 glass red wine
1 T. sugar
1/2 stick cinnamon
Salt and pepper to taste

1.  Remove wilted leaves from cabbage. Cut head in half and remove center.
2.  Very finely shred cabbage.  Pour boiling broth over it, add butter and cook for 1 hour.
3.  Add remaining ingredients and continue cooking for 1/2 hour, turning frequently.
4.  Ten minutes before serving, add 1/2 glass of red wine and finish cooking.


NOTE:  Cooked cabbage should be neither too sour nor too sweet.



***For dessert I recommend that you serve your favorite soft dessert cheese with either apples or sliced winter pears.***

### The
# Blue Fox

*Dinner for Six*

*Vitello Tonnato*
*(Veal Tonne)*

*Belgian Endive and Watercress Salad*

*Boneless Loin of Lamb, Verdi*

*Strawberries Armagnac*

*Wine:*

*With Vitello Tonnato—Trefethen Vineyards*
*Chardonnay, 1974*
*or Fontana Candida Frascati Secco, 1976*

*With Lamb—Stag's Leap Wine Cellars Petite Sirah, 1973*
*or Chapoutier Châteauneuf-du-Pape, 1964*

*With Strawberries—Almadén Vineyards Johannisberg*
*Riesling, Late Harvest, 1975*
*or Saulheimer Probstey,*
*Trockenbeerenauslese, Orig. Abf. Karl Kissel, 1971*

*Mario Mondin, Owner*

*Walter Sturzenegger, Head Chef*

It has been said that the finest San Francisco restaurants can be found in dark alleys and on side streets. The Blue Fox is one of those restaurants, located on Merchant Street. When the city morgue and the jail moved it lost its slogan, *"Across the street from the morgue"*.

The name and logo come from the blue fox which is a summer color phase of the white or Arctic fox. Mario Mondin, owner since 1942, began in the restaurant business as a busboy, dishwasher and bartender. His Blue Fox guests have included many well-known politicians and performers. "This is my house," he says. "I still work fourteen hours a day, but I'm too temperamental to be a chef. I believe that one must dedicate himself completely."

The famous wine cellars are available for private parties. The original party was held one night when some waiting customers were asked if they wouldn't mind having dinner at the large table down in the wine cellar. Public demand has resulted in the building of wine cellar additions.

The Blue Fox's head chef Walter Sturzenegger has been cooking for thirty years and learned his art in Switzerland. "Cooking is serious business," he says. "Recipes should be carefully followed."

## VITELLO TONNATO

***This is Mario Mondin's recipe and it is over thirty years old.
This is a classic dish from Turin, served in Italy on state occasions.
We are the only restaurant in San Francisco to make it. Be certain not to overdo the anchovies in the sauce. It is important to
maintain the tuna flavor.***

1½ lb. loin of veal, free of fat and sinew
3 stalks celery
1 medium onion
1 medium carrot
3 cloves
3 qts. rich chicken stock
Cheesecloth and string

1. Put veal in cheesecloth and roll into the form of a sausage. Fasten
both ends with string and place three ties in between.
2. Place the veal in a pot with the remaining ingredients. Bring to a
boil and let simmer for 1½ hours, keeping the pan covered while
cooking.
3. Remove veal from pot and place under a weight to extract the
moisture. Let stand until cool and then place in the refrigerator
until firm. Do not remove cloth until ready to serve. Serve with Veal
Sauce.

## VEAL SAUCE

1/2 large dill pickle
4 stalks celery
1 small green onion
2 t. capers
6 oz. tuna
8 anchovy fillets
2 oz. lemon juice
1 qt. homemade mayonnaise
Salt and white pepper to taste
Whole capers (garnish)

1. Put pickle, celery, onion, capers, tuna and anchovies through a food grinder or in a blender and make a fine purée.
2. Place mayonnaise in a mixing bowl. Add purée and lemon juice. Season with salt and pepper. Mix with a whip until well blended.

## TO SERVE:

Cut veal into thin slices. Arrange slightly overlapping slices on a platter. Spread generously with sauce. Sprinkle with whole capers and serve.

NOTE: You may also decorate with sliced olives, thin pimento, anchovy curls or thin slices of hard-boiled egg.

BELGIAN ENDIVE AND WATERCRESS SALAD

6 heads Belgian endive
Few sprigs watercress
Sprinkle of chopped parsley
Olive oil
Wine vinegar
Salt
Pepper

1. Wash and dry endive. Cut into quarters lengthwise.
2. Arrange 4 quarters on individual salad dishes, adding a few sprigs of clean watercress. Just before serving sprinkle with chopped parsley and add salad dressing.

NOTE: "At The Blue Fox we often serve this topped with fresh baby shrimp or fresh crab legs. In either case the shrimp or crab is first marinated in the dressing mixture for two hours. This could be used either as a first course or as a luncheon salad. For a hearty luncheon one could add thinly sliced cold chicken or cold boiled beef. It's a great way to use leftovers."

***A fine dinner depends on more than cooking.
Timing and how the food is served are also important.
Plates should be the proper temperature—chilled for cold foods, warmed for hot—and the food should be attractively served.***

### BONELESS LOIN OF LAMB, VERDI

\*\*\*This was developed by our chef about one year ago.\*\*\*

2½ to 3 lbs. loin of lamb (about 3 loins), trimmed of all fat and sinew
5 T. butter
2 cups mirepoix au maigre (diced celery, carrots, onions)
1 clove garlic
1 t. whole rosemary
1/3 cup cognac
2 cups Asti wine
2 cups beef stock
1 T. meat glaze
Salt
Freshly cracked black pepper
Small Belgian carrots, cooked
Parisienne potatoes, cooked
6 artichoke bottoms
Chestnut purée
12 mushroom caps
4 oz. pâté de foie gras
3 loaves unsliced white bread
Watercress
Parsley
Cornstarch (optional)
Oil

1. Preheat oven to 375°.
2. Heat 2 T. butter in a large, heavy pan. Add meat and brown well.
3. Heat cognac in a small pan. Ignite and pour over the meat. Remove the meat from the pan and set aside.
4. Add the mirepoix, crushed garlic and rosemary to the pan and cook over low heat for 3 minutes.
5. Remove from heat and add meat glaze. Add wine and beef stock and season with salt and pepper. Stir the sauce over low heat until it comes to a boil.
6. Return the meat to the pan and let it braise, uncovered, in the oven for 20 to 25 minutes.

7. When the meat is cooked, remove it from the pan and boil the sauce down to about two-thirds quantity, thickening with cornstarch if necessary. Strain.

8. Brown the potatoes and heat the carrots in butter. Sauté mushrooms.

9. Put chestnut purée in a pastry bag and place a rosette in the artichoke bottoms. Place in oven until hot.

10. Remove crust from bread and scoop out a section along the top of each loaf to form a 'shoe'. Deep-fry.

11. Mount the loins on the bread 'shoes' and top with thinly sliced pâté and sautéed mushroom caps.

12. Garnish the platter with the potatoes and carrots. Sprinkle with parsley and add the stuffed artichoke bottoms and a pinch of watercress. Serve immediately and carve the meat at the table. Serve sauce in a separate bowl.

## STRAWBERRIES ARMAGNAC

***Marinate the berries from two hours to overnight but no longer or they will be mushy.***

4 oz. sherry
4 oz. port
2 oz. Armagnac
1/2 cup granulated sugar
2 baskets strawberries
6 small scoops vanilla ice cream
Whipped cream

1. Mix together sherry, port, Armagnac and sugar until the sugar dissolves.

2. Clean and slice strawberries. Set aside 6 whole berries. Marinate the remaining strawberries in the above mixture.

3. Serve berries in a large glass bowl. Serve 1 scoop of ice cream per person. Arrange strawberries around circumference of ice cream, add liquid and top with a rosette of whipped cream and 1 whole strawberry.

*Dinner for Six*


*Sashimi*

*Sunomono*

*Tempura*

*Sesame Chicken*

*Beef Sukiyaki*

*Steamed Rice*

*Fresh Fruit*


*Wine:*
*Sake or White Wine such as Chenin Blanc or Chablis*


*Ryozo (Joe), Koichi (Kobo), and Kenzi (Ken)*
*Ishizaki, Owners*

*Kobo Ishizaki, Executive Chef*

San Francisco's oldest Japanese restaurant, founded in 1946 as Pacific Sukiyaki by the Ishizaki family, is a favorite of the western and Japanese communities. It became Yamato when it moved to Nob Hill in 1950. Yamato means "Mountain Gate" in Japanese.

"The restaurant reflects classic Japanese cuisine with the basic types of food: tempura, sashimi, sukiyaki, and teriyaki," says Joe Ishizaki. "We serve the best food available. All the details are important too: the decor, creatively arranged plates, kimonoed waitresses. Even the restrooms should be cleaner than a person's home. This is my home and I like to see things right. Dining out is an adventure for people. Our prime motive is to take good care of them and enhance their evening."

Ishizaki has cooked for seventeen years and believes that cooking should be fun and not a big project. "If you make anything work, it becomes a chore and then it's not fun. The secret is in the preparation. I still cook everything from corned beef and cabbage to lamb or roast beef for my friends. Restaurateurs are dedicated people."

The dedication at Yamato's is clear from the Holiday Magazine Dining Awards and the Mobil Travel Guide Four-Star Award they have received. On the occasion of Emperor Hirohito's visit, Yamato was chosen to prepare the food for His Majesty and his staff and received a special award from Japan Airlines.

SASHIMI

***The fresher the fish, the better the taste. Be careful not to
handle the fish with your hands or it will pick up a salty taste.
Each slice of fish should have sharp edges, so a good knife is essential. The knives we use in our kitchen are made in the same way as
a samurai sword.***

1 lb. fresh fish—tuna, halibut, striped bass or perch, but no salmon
Soy sauce
Wasabi (Japanese green horseradish)
Colman's Dry Mustard
Lemon

1. Clean fish and remove skin. "If you are using cold water tuna remember that the most tender part is the belly. We call this part 'toro'."
2. Cut fish into squares and then slice into rectangles. The thickness
of the pieces will depend on the tenderness of the fish but the slices
should not be more than 3/4 inch thick.
3. Mix mustard with water to form a sauce. Mix wasabi with water.
Allow both mixtures to stand for a few minutes.
4. Serve fish with lemon, soy sauce, mustard and horseradish.

***Using chopsticks is not as hard as you might think. They will de-
finitely enhance the meal.***

***There are different types of soy sauce. The heavy kind is usually
used for sashimi and the light type for foods you don't want to discolor.
Soy sauce should never be poured over food like ketchup. Remember
to season foods lightly. You should be able to pick out the subtle
flavors of each dish.***

### SUNOMONO

1½ lb. cucumbers, peeled and thinly sliced
3/4 t. salt
3/4 cup cider vinegar
1/2 cup sugar
3/4 t. MSG
Garnish: cooked crab, shrimp, tomato slices

1. Sprinkle cucumbers with salt. Allow to stand at room temperature for 1 hour.
2. Thoroughly blend together remaining ingredients, stirring until sugar dissolves.
3. Add 3/8 cup of the vinegar sauce to the cucumbers. Stir lightly and drain. Just before serving pour remaining dressing over cucumbers. Serve in individual bowls and garnish with cooked crab, shrimp and tomato slices.

### TEMPURA

***The color of tempura comes from the oil rather than the batter. The secret of good color is in using a blend of new and used oil. Never cook too much food at once or the oil temperature will be lowered. The tempura should never be soggy. Hot or cold, the batter should be crisp.***

1/2 lb. fish fillets, cut into 1½ X 2 inch pieces
12 raw shrimp or prawns, cleaned and butterflied (leave tails on)
6 raw scallops (if large, cut in half and skewer on wood or toothpick)
1 green pepper cut in 1½ X 2 inch pieces
1 sweet potato (peeled) or 3 carrots (peeled) cut diagonally into 1/4
        inch slices
1 small eggplant or 2 average zucchini, unpeeled and cut into 1/4 inch
        slices
1/4 lb. green beans or asparagus tips, cut into bite-sized pieces
Vegetable oil for frying

## BATTER

3 cups sifted cake flour
1 T. baking powder
2 egg yolks
2 cups ice-cold water

1. Drain seafood and vegetables thoroughly on paper towels. Arrange on a large platter.
2. Pour oil at least 2 inches deep into an electric fry pan or deep, wide fry pan. Heat oil to 370°. If you don't have a thermometer test oil by dropping a piece of vegetable into the pan. It should float.
3. Sift flour and baking powder.
4. Thoroughly beat egg yolks with a wire whisk or hand beater (rotary, not electric). Blend in water.
5. Sprinkle all of the flour mixture evenly over the liquid. Use a whisk or beater to stir in flour quickly until it is moistened and large lumps disappear. Batter should be very lumpy and the consistency of whipping cream. *Do not stir batter after it is mixed.*
6. Coat ingredients with batter, starting with shrimp. Slightly drain off excess batter and slide the food into the hot oil. Fry about 1 minute. Turn over and fry 1 minute longer or until cooked a light golden brown. Dip and fry other ingredients in the same manner. Skim off bits of cooked batter. Drain on paper towels or a wire rack and serve with Tempura Sauce.

## TEMPURA SAUCE

1/2 cup dashi (Japanese fish stock)
1/4 cup Kikkoman Soy Sauce
2 t. sugar
MSG (dash)

Combine all ingredients in a saucepan. Heat until warm.

NOTE: Kikkoman Tempura Sauce may be substituted. Follow label directions.

## TO SERVE TEMPURA:

Line a small bowl with a paper towel or an open basket with paper. In each, place an assortment of all the tempura items along with a container of the tempura sauce. Dip each piece in sauce before eating. "Note variety in texture and taste."

### SESAME CHICKEN

***Remember not to marinate the chicken too long or it might be too salty.***

1/4 cup Kikkoman Soy Sauce
2 T. sugar
2 T. sake (Japanese rice wine) or dry sherry
1/2 t. grated fresh ginger or powdered ginger
2¼ pound chicken, cut into 1½ inch pieces (do not use back)—bone-
     less chicken may be used
1/4 cup cornstarch
1 T. toasted sesame seeds
2 cups oil
Hot mustard

1.  Blend soy sauce, sugar, sake and ginger. Add chicken pieces and marinate 30 to 40 minutes.
2.  Combine cornstarch and sesame seeds. Place mixture in a paper bag.
3.  Remove chicken from marinade. Drop chicken pieces in cornstarch/sesame mixture and let stand for 10 minutes.
4.  Heat oil to 350-375°. Fry chicken to golden brown, about 4 minutes (or slightly longer for chicken with bone), until done. Serve with additional soy sauce and hot mustard.

***Most people cook rice incorrectly. I would recommend an electric rice cooker because once you have the proper proportion of rice and water you will never have to worry.***

## BEEF SUKIYAKI

***This is one of our most popular dishes. If you don't have all of the following ingredients, feel free to improvise. You can cook this dish at the table.***

1½ to 2 lbs. boneless beef top sirloin or rib steak, as thinly sliced as possible
2 bunches green onions, cut into 1½ inch lengths
4 medium onions, sliced into chunks (1/6ths)
1 cake tofu (soybean curd), cut into 1 inch cubes
1 can (8½ oz.) bamboo shoots, sliced
1/2 lb. fresh bean sprouts
3/4 lb. fresh mushrooms, sliced
4 stalks celery, cut diagonally into 1/2 inch slices
1 can (8½ oz.) shirataki
2 pieces beef suet or 1 T. salad oil

## SUKIYAKI SAUCE

1/2 cup Kikkoman Soy Sauce
1/4 cup condensed consommé or beef broth
1/4 cup water
1 T. sugar
2 T. sake

1. Arrange beef and vegetables attractively on a large platter.
2. Prepare sauce by combining ingredients in a saucepan and stirring until sugar dissolves. (You can substitute with 1¼ cups Kikkoman Sukiyaki Sauce.)
3. Heat an electric skillet to 300° or heat a large, heavy fry pan. Melt suet in skillet (or heat oil), stirring until pan is well coated. Remove suet.
4. Add half of the meat and sear until brown. Add half of the vegetables and half of the sauce. Keep meat and vegetables separate. Cook only until the vegetables are tender, yet crisp. Serve immediately in individual bowls or plates. Refill skillet with remaining ingredients and follow same procedure.

NOTE: Mushrooms and shirataki may be replaced by 2 cans (8¾ oz. each) or sukiyaki-no-tomo.

**THE MANDARIN**

*Dinner for Four to Six*

*Stuffed Cucumber Soup*

*Chicken Livers Sauté*

*Beggar's Chicken*

*Eggplant and Pork Szechwan Style*

*Steamed Rice*

*Glacéed Bananas*

*Wine:*

*A Dry or Fruity White Wine*

*Especially recommended with Eggplant
and Pork— Gewürztraminer*

*Cecilia Chiang, Owner
Tony Ming Chan, Head Chef*

Cecilia Chiang opened the original Mandarin at a time when few people were familiar with Peking or Northern Chinese cuisine. "Everyone thought I was crazy," she says. Her business was so successful that she moved it to Ghirardelli Square and opened a second Mandarin in Beverly Hills. She commutes twice weekly to both restaurants and believes in close supervision in everything from marketing to food preparation to decor.

The Mandarin serves the kind of food Mme. Chiang knows best and likes to eat most: the classic dishes from Shanghai, where she was born, from Peking, where she grew up, and from the provinces of Hunan and Szechwan. She was one of the first to serve Szechwan food in this country.

The Mandarin has received many Holiday Magazine Awards as well as the Mobil Travel Guide Four-Star Award.

Head chef Tony Ming Chan was born in Canton, China. At the age of twenty he began to study cooking in Hong Kong under Chan Winn, a renowned chef and author of many cookbooks. Chan came to San Francisco in 1966 and worked in various Chinese restaurants before joining The Mandarin.

## STUFFED CUCUMBER SOUP

3 large cucumbers
4 cups clear chicken stock
A sprinkle of fresh coriander (Chinese parsley), chopped or a sprinkle
    of green onion tops, chopped
1/3 cup cooked prawns, finely chopped
1/3 cup lean uncooked pork, finely chopped
1/3 cup fresh raw Chinese cabbage, chopped
A little fresh ginger root, grated
A few green onion tops, finely sliced or chopped
A little fresh coriander (Chinese parsley), chopped
1 T. sesame oil
Soy sauce
Salt
1 to 2 T. clear chicken stock

1.  Prepare filling by blending the prawns, pork and Chinese cabbage.
Add ginger root, onions and coriander and mix well.
2.  Add sesame oil.  Add soy sauce and/or salt to taste.
3.  Cover and place in refrigerator for at least 1 hour so flavors will
blend.  Just before using, add enough chicken stock to moisten the mixture without making it soggy.
4.  Peel cucumbers and cut in half lengthwise.  Scoop out seeds and pulp.
5.  Place filling in hollowed cucumber centers.
6.  Cut crosswise in 2 inch pieces.  Chill thoroughly.
7.  Steam slices 20 to 30 minutes.  Do not overcook or cucumber will
lose its shape and consistency.
8.  Heat chicken stock.  Just before serving, place cucumber slices into
broth and simmer until filling is cooked through.  Serve in hot bowls
with a sprinkle of coriander or green onion.

## CHICKEN LIVERS SAUTÉ

1-1/3 lbs. chicken livers
4 scallions
1 ginger root
3 to 4 T. cottonseed oil
1 T. soy sauce
1/2 t. sugar
Sesame oil (few drops)
White pepper (dash)
A few splashes of sherry
1 T. oyster sauce
2 T. chicken stock
2 T. cornstarch/water solution

1. Rinse chicken livers in cold water and drain. Trim well, removing veins and membranes. Slice into thirds.
2. Blanch livers in boiling water for 40 to 50 seconds. Remove with strainer.
3. Diagonally slice white part of scallions into 2 inch segments. Rinse in cold water.
4. Peel ginger and cut into 10 to 12 very thin slices.
5. Heat wok over high temperature. Coat inside surface with cottonseed oil.
6. Add scallions and ginger. Toss and stir for 1 minute.
7. Add chicken livers, continuing to toss and stir. Add remaining ingredients. Toss and stir for a few seconds before serving.

NOTE: Remember that the total cooking time, exclusive of blanching, is only about 1½ minutes.

## BEGGAR'S CHICKEN

***The Mandarin was the first restaurant in America to serve this dish.***

1 chicken, about 3 lbs.
1 T. sherry
1½ t. salt
1/2 t. 5-spice powder
1/2 t. sesame oil
1/2 T. soy sauce
8 to 10 slices water chestnuts
3 to 4 slices Virginia ham, cut julienne
20 slices Chinese black mushrooms, presoaked
20 slices bamboo shoots, cut julienne
Ceramic clay (found in art supply stores)
A brown paper bag
Aluminum foil

1. Wash chicken and pat dry. Rub the outside and cavity with sherry
and a mixture of the salt, 5-spice powder and sesame oil and soy sauce.
2. Combine water chestnuts, ham, mushrooms and bamboo shoots.
Stuff the chicken with the mixture.
3. Wrap the chicken in 2 layers of foil and place in the paper bag.
4. Mix the ceramic clay with enough water to form a thick, spreadable
consistency.
5. Tightly fold the paper bag around the chicken and encase it with a
1/4 inch layer of wet clay. Place on a cookie sheet.
6. Bake in a preheated 450° oven for 1½ hours. Reduce temperature to
300° and bake for an additional 45 minutes.
7. To serve, crack clay with a mallet and open paper. Meat should fall
off the bones. (Larger bones can be removed for easier serving.) Serve
with Beggar's Chicken Sauce.

BEGGAR'S CHICKEN SAUCE

1 cup chicken stock
1 T. cottonseed oil
1 T. sherry
1/2 t. sugar
A sprinkle of MSG
1 T. soy sauce
1 T. oyster sauce
A few drops of sesame oil
2 T. cornstarch/water solution

Cook for several minutes until the mixture is fairly thick.  Ladle over the chicken.

***Correct preparation of vegetables is very important in Chinese cuisine.  Vegetables should *not* be overcooked.  Remember, too, to cut all sliced food on the bias rather than straight across.  Try practicing on celery tops or other wastage.***

***The difference between Mandarin cooking and Cantonese cuisine is that Mandarin food is more flavorful.  Also, Cantonese cooking uses starch or grease and is heavier.***

## EGGPLANT AND PORK SZECHWAN STYLE

***This is one of the ten courses served at the Celestial Feast to celebrate Chinese New Year at The Mandarin.***

2 medium eggplants
1/2 lb. pork butt, chopped semi-finely
1 large clove garlic, sliced thinly
2 scallions (about 5 inches of white part), finely minced
Oil for cooking
2 t. hot bean paste
1 cup chicken stock
1 T. hoisin sauce
1 T. vinegar
1 T. pepper corn oil
1 T. hot chili pepper oil
1 T. sherry
2 t. sugar
1/2 t. sesame oil
2 T. cornstarch/water solution

1. Peel eggplants. Cut each into 6 long pieces and cut diagonally into 1½ inch chunks.
2. Quick-stir ("chow") the eggplants with a little oil. Set aside on a large platter.
3. Heat 2 T. oil in a wok to a high temperature. Add garlic and brown. Add pork.
4. While stirring, add bean paste, chicken stock, hoisin sauce, vinegar, pepper corn oil and hot chili pepper oil.
5. Add the scallions and, still stirring, the sherry and sugar.
6. Return the eggplant and quick-stir over high heat for about 2 minutes.
7. Stir in sesame oil and cornstarch/water mixture. Remove from heat and serve immediately.

## GLACÉED BANANAS

3 semi-ripe bananas
All-purpose flour for coating
2 egg whites
1-1/3 cups water
1/2 cup flour
1 cup sugar
1/4 cup oil
1 to 1½ qts. oil for frying
A large bowl of water with ice cubes
A pair of tongs or serving spoons

1.  Peel and cut bananas on the bias into 4 pieces each. Coat with flour and set aside.
2.  Combine egg whites, 1/3 cup water and 1/2 cup flour in a large bowl, to make batter.
3.  In a wok prepare a syrup made of sugar, 1 cup water and 1/4 cup oil. Heat until the syrup forms a hard ball when a drop is submerged in cold water.
4.  At the same time, heat oil for frying in a second wok. Bring to a temperature of approximately 375°.

5. Coat bananas with batter and drop into the oil to deep-fry for about 30 seconds or until a light golden brown.

6. Remove bananas with a strainer and place in the syrup, stirring to make sure that the bananas are completely covered with syrup. Quickly transfer the fruit to a serving plate which is coated with oil.

7. Moving quickly, drop each piece of banana into the ice water. The syrup will turn into a crisp, candy-like shell. Serve immediately.

***'Mandarin' really refers to the type of food eaten by the Mandarin classes in China. This type of cuisine includes Peking dishes and specialties from all over China. Classic dishes come from Peking, Shanghai and from the provinces of Hunan and Szechwan where the food can be so hot that your hair stands straight up. The restaurant's cooking is not *that* spicy.***

*Dinner for Four to Six*

*Marinated Prawns*

*Tortellini Vincent Price*

*Abalone Speciale de la Casa*

*Fresh Fruit Crêpe*

*Café Amaretto*

*Wine:*

*With Tortellini—Robert Mondavi Fumé Blanc,
Napa Valley, 1975*

*With Abalone—Louis Jadot Chevalier-Montrachet,
Les Domiciles, 1972*

*With Crêpe—Robert Mondavi Moscato d'Oro
(Serve extremely chilled—almost frozen)*

*Frances "Mama" and Michael "Papa" Sanchez, Owners*

*Salvatore Di Grande, Head Chef*

The dishes at Mama's in the Grosvenor Towers on Nob Hill are those that owners Frances 'Mama' and Michael 'Papa' Sanchez cook at home for family and friends.

Fresh is the key word here whether in the flower arrangements or food. Glass cases display fruits, salads, cakes and pastries. "If it's out of season, we take it off the menu," says Mr. Sanchez.

The first Mama's started in the North Beach area in 1969. It was followed by another in the 'cellar' at Macy's, and in 1976, by the one in the Grosvenor Towers. Other Mama's are located in San Mateo, Palo Alto and San Jose.

"To be a good restaurant you must continuously serve quality food. The proof is not only in being good but in getting better and better. I hope a year from now we'll be twice as good as we are now. If you own a restaurant you must be around to see that everything is right. I'm here every night to taste the food."

Head chef Salvatore Di Grande says, "People like food with body and flavor." He has been cooking for thirty years and joined Mama's in 1975. "My father loved to cook around the house in Italy and when I was a teenager I watched him prepare food. My mother also really knows how to cook. I'm very happy. The way we work here is just like a family. I even sing in the kitchen."

## MARINATED PRAWNS

***If fish and seafood are fresh there will be no odor in the kitchen.***

### PRAWNS

1/2 lb. prawns
Salt
Pepper
1 lemon, cut in small pieces

1.  Remove all the shell except the last small segment or tail. With a sharp knife slit each prawn down the back and lift out the black or white intestinal vein. Wash prawns quickly under cold water.
2.  Boil in hot water with salt, pepper and lemon for about 10 minutes.
3.  Strain. Place in a salad bowl and mix with Prawn Marinade. Marinate for 5 to 6 hours or overnight.

### PRAWN MARINADE

***The longer you marinate the better the flavor.***

1 cup olive oil
1/3 cup red wine vinegar
1 t. salt
1 t. ground pepper
2 T. green onions, chopped
2 T. parsley, chopped
1 T. lemon juice
2 cloves garlic, finely chopped
1 t. sugar
Oregano (pinch)

Combine all ingredients.

## TORTELLINI VINCENT PRICE

***One day Vincent Price came to our restaurant and asked if we could prepare tortellini with prosciutto. This is a basic Italian dish but I've added my own touch of a little bit of pesto which changes the flavor and makes the food look so beautiful that you want to eat it right away. Vincent Price liked it so much that we decided to name the dish after him.***

6 to 7 tortellini per person

## CREAM SAUCE PROSCIUTTO

8 T. butter
8 T. all-purpose flour
2 t. salt
1/3 t. white pepper
2 cups light cream
1/2 cup heavy cream
1/3 t. nutmeg
1 T. pesto
2 T. Parmesan cheese, freshly grated
4 to 6 slices prosciutto, thinly sliced, rolled and cut julienne

1. Melt butter in a small saucepan.
2. Remove from heat and add flour, stirring constantly. Return pan to low heat and cook slightly, being careful not to brown the flour.
3. Remove pan from heat and add cream, salt and pepper. Return to low heat, stirring gently until near boiling.
4. Add Parmesan cheese, pesto, nutmeg and prosciutto. Simmer for 2 to 3 minutes.
5. Boil tortellini.
6. Place tortellini in the sauce and let set for 1 to 2 minutes to pick up the flavor of the sauce. Serve.

## ABALONE SPECIALE DE LA CASA

***Cook the abalone no more than thirty seconds per side. Overcooking will make it tough. Also make sure that your butter is not too hot.***

2 to 3 slices abalone per person
Flour
Eggs
Butter
Lemon juice
Salt
Pepper

1. Slice abalone very thinly.
2. Dip each slice in flour and beaten eggs.
3. Pan-fry in butter with a touch of lemon juice, salt and pepper.

***Frozen fish is not the same as fresh because too much water is retained from the cold. When the fish is defrosted and fried, the excess water will change the texture. If you must use frozen fish, at least be sure to defrost it at room temperature.***

## FRESH FRUIT CRÊPE

\*\*\*Fruit will keep better if it is handled carefully. Be gentle, especially with apples and bananas. Bananas should not be stored in the refrigerator or they will become soggy. If you ever want a cold one, chill it for about thirty minutes. Other fruits and vegetables will stay fresh for one to two days if they are kept in plastic bags in the refrigerator.\*\*\*

## CRÊPE

4 eggs
1/2 cup flour
1/2 t. cinnamon
3 T. sugar
Salt (pinch)
1½ cups light cream
5 T. melted butter plus 1/2 t. butter
5 drops vanilla

1. Beat eggs.
2. Add flour, cinnamon, sugar, and salt.
3. Gradually stir in cream, 5 T. melted butter and vanilla. Beat the mixture for 30 seconds. Let batter rest for 20 minutes.
4. Slowly heat omelette pan over low heat. Add 1/2 t. butter and swirl pan to coat bottom with butter.
5. Pour in about 2 to 3 T. crêpe batter. Immediately swirl pan to coat bottom with a thin film. Let cook until light brown on underside. Carefully turn with a spatula and let brown on the other side. Batter will make 12 crêpes, 6 to 8 inches in diameter.

## FRESH FRUIT FILLING

***Any type of jam may be substituted for the orange marmalade.  I sometimes even substitute a chocolate cream.***

1 apple
1 banana
1/2 cup strawberries
6 T. orange marmalade
12 T. raspberry jam
1½ T. Grand Marnier
Powdered sugar

1.  Peel and core apple.  Peel banana and hull and wash strawberries. Chop apple, banana and strawberries into very small pieces.
2.  Spread 1 T. orange marmalade on each crêpe.
3.  Fill crêpe with 1 T. chopped fruit.  Roll and place on serving dish.
4.  In a small crêpe pan melt raspberry jam with Grand Marnier.  When melted and hot, spoon over crêpes.
5.  Sprinkle lightly with powdered sugar and serve at once.

## CAFÉ AMARETTO

Per person:

1½ oz. Amaretto di Saronno
5 to 5½ oz. coffee
Whipped cream
Ground nutmeg

1.  Mix coffee and liqueur in a tall fluted glass.
2.  Add cream which has been whipped just enough to float on top. Top with a sprinkle of nutmeg.

# SAM'S GRILL

*Dinner for Four*

*Mock Turtle Soup*

*Sam's Special Salad*

*Clams Elizabeth*

*French Fried Zucchini*

*French Pancakes, Anisette*

*Wine:*

*Wente Brothers Grey Riesling or Sauvignon Blanc*

*Frank, Walter and Gary Seput, Owners*

*Fritz Schneider, Head Chef*

The history of Sam's Grill goes back to 1867 when it first opened as The Bay Point Oyster Bar. Sam later took over and in 1937 the late elder Frank Seput bought the restaurant. Since then three generations of Seputs have been actively involved.

Grandson Gary says,"We haven't changed much. We try to perpetuate the old San Francisco style and tradition. Many of the dishes are from my grandfather's recipes.

"We're involved in everything and even go to the market every day. We still do many things by hand. We're proud of this policy and are going to maintain it."

Chef Fritz Schneider started working in China and came to the United States in 1948. He has been cooking at Sam's Grill for eighteen years. He and Walter Seput agree that diners appreciate food more now. "We have a wider spectrum of people coming to the restaurant than in the past."

MOCK TURTLE SOUP

***This recipe is from the original Sam's.***

4 cups chicken broth
4 oz. tomato purée
3 T. chicken fat
3 T. sifted flour
Ground allspice (dash)
Ground cloves (dash)
1/4 t. salt
1 shot glass Burgundy
1 shot glass cherry wine
Skin from a boiled chicken
Juice of 1/2 medium lemon
2 hard-boiled eggs
Accent (dash)

1. Mix broth with tomato purée. Bring mixture to a boil.
2. Heat chicken fat and add flour. Stir until smooth.
3. Pour boiling broth over fat/flour mixture and beat constantly until smooth.
4. Add allspice, cloves and wines. Blend well.
5. Pass eggs and chicken skin through a grinder and add ingredients to soup.
6. Add salt, Accent and lemon juice. Mix well, bring to a boil and serve.

***The secret of cooking fish is in controlling the heat inside the pan. When sautéeing, use a little oil with the butter to prevent the butter from burning. Also remember that adding more ingredients will cool the temperature inside the pan.***

## SAM'S SPECIAL SALAD

2 celery hearts
2 tomatoes, sliced
1 avocado, cut into strips
1/2 lb. shrimp or crab meat
Fresh parsley

1. Slowly boil celery hearts until tender. Remove from heat. Leave hearts in some of the juice and chill.
2. Cut celery hearts into 4 halves and place one on each salad plate. (You may also cut into 4 strips for easier eating.) Garnish on each side with a slice of tomato.
3. Place avocado strips sideways, about 1 inch apart on celery and fill with shellfish.
4. Spoon Blue Cheese Dressing on top and sprinkle with fresh parsley just before serving.

## BLUE CHEESE DRESSING (1 pint)

3 oz. wedge of blue cheese
1/4 t. salt
1/8 t. black pepper
1/8 t. Colman's Dry Mustard
1½ oz. red wine vinegar
6 oz. salad oil or olive oil

1. Mix dry ingredients in a bowl. Slowly add vinegar, stirring well.
2. Add oil and mix.
3. In a separate bowl, mash blue cheese with a dinner fork.
4. Add dressing to cheese, stirring well from bottom up. Add more vinegar to taste to compensate for oil from cheese. Serve.

## CLAMS ELIZABETH

***This is an original recipe developed by the late Frank Seput.  I
don't know of any other restaurant which serves anything like it.***

4 dozen medium clams, raw
3 T. chives or scallions, finely chopped
8 T. fine white bread crumbs
4 T. Parmesan cheese, grated
Juice of 3 lemons
8 T. melted butter
8 oz. sherry
Paprika

1.  Use any clams which are in season.  Open and leave on the half-shell.
Reserve the juice.
2.  Place the clams in a shallow baking dish and add the juice.
3.  Mix bread crumbs with Parmesan cheese and chives or scallions.
4.  Sprinkle lemon juice over each clam.  Sprinkle bread crumb/cheese
mixture over clams.
5.  Top with melted butter and cover very lightly with paprika.  Bake
in a hot oven (400°) for 20 minutes or until brown.

***Most of our recipes are simple.  We don't cover our food with sauces.
When cooking at home be careful not to overspice.  Timing is also very
important.  When broiling fish it is better to remove the food from the
broiler when it is a tiny bit rare.  The heat of the fish will finish the
cooking and the inside will be nice and moist.***

***There is a lot of instinct involved in knowing when your fish is
done and a sense of smell has a good deal to do with this instinct.***

FRENCH FRIED ZUCCHINI

***We use French bread crumbs for this recipe.***

4 medium zucchini, sliced julienne
Bread crumbs
3 large eggs
1/2 cup milk
Oil

1. Beat eggs.  Add milk.
2. Dip zucchini into the egg/milk mixture and bread them.
3. Heat oil to 400°.  Add breaded zucchini and cook approximately 10 minutes.

***To be a good cook you need a good parking place, a happy home life and good ingredients.***

## FRENCH PANCAKES, ANISETTE

1 cup sifted flour
1/2 t. sugar
Salt (pinch)
1 cup milk
2 T. melted butter
2 eggs, beaten
1 oz. anisette

1. Sift the flour and salt into a mixing bowl.
2. Add sugar, milk, melted butter and eggs and beat until very smooth. Batter should be the consistency of thick cream. Let sit 30 to 40 minutes.
3. Heat a small skillet and grease it very lightly. Pour about 1 T. of the batter into the skillet and tilt the pan swiftly to spread the batter evenly. Cook until lightly browned on the bottom, for about 1/2 minute. Turn and brown other side. Fold pancakes on a plate.
4. Pour anisette over the folded pancakes.

Dinner Menu

GOLDEN EAGLE

one sixty california street · san francisco · yukon two·eight·eight·three·one

*Dinner for Four to Six*

*Sauerkraut Soup*

*Hearts of Romaine Salad with Blue Cheese Dressing*

*Fisherman's Prawns*

*Buttered Rice*

*Coeur à la Crème*

*Wine:*
*With Prawns — Robert Mondavi Fumé Blanc*
*With Coeur à la Crème — Asti Spumante*

*George Patterson and Jon Hadley, Owners*
*Jon Hadley, Head Chef*

In 1969, native San Franciscans George Patterson and Jon Hadley opened The Golden Eagle in the city's financial district. "Our idea was to design a restaurant that represented the San Francisco of fifty or sixty years ago; where people could leave their offices and relax in a club-like atmosphere," says Jon Hadley.

"We found a stuffed golden eagle, when it was legal to buy one, and then found an 1890 eagle plate which was used to print stocks and bonds. We made a logo from it for the menu and the restaurant became 'The Golden Eagle'." George Patterson maintains the business end of the restaurant; Hadley runs the kitchen.

Hadley started cooking at age twelve by watching his mother, who owned her own restaurant. Further training included cooking while in college and "watching Julia Child". The recipes used at the restaurant are all his personal favorites. The Golden Eagle makes its own homemade ice cream and has invented some flavors.

"I like the business," continues Hadley. "This is a set, the closest thing there is to the theater without being in it . . .it's a performance all the time."

## SAUERKRAUT SOUP

***I developed this recipe seven years ago. The important thing to remember when preparing soup is that ingredients vary from place to place and from time to time. No two batches will ever come out the same. Every morning at the restaurant we hold at least two tastings to balance the flavors and season properly. With this recipe be sure to wash the sauerkraut once to remove some of the vinegar. This will prevent the soup from being too sour. A good texture is maintained by placing only half of the mixture in the blender. Also, since some sauerkraut is saltier than others the salt should be added after the soup has simmered and the flavors have all blended. The soup should be sweet and sour.***

3/4 lb. hamburger
3 T. butter
1 stalk celery, finely chopped
2½ size can sauerkraut, rinsed once, drained and finely chopped
2 onions, finely chopped
2 qts. beef stock
1 qt. water
1 small bay leaf
1 t. Worcestershire sauce
1/4 t. dill weed
2 t. salt
1/4 t. pepper
2 T. sugar
Sour cream

1. Sauté hamburger separately and drain off any fat.
2. Sauté the vegetables (except sauerkraut) in butter until soft.
3. Blend the meat into the vegetables and add the stock, sauerkraut and water. Flavor with bay leaf, dill weed and pepper. Simmer for 45 minutes.
4. Put half of the soup, including half of the sauerkraut, through a food mill or a blender and return to pot.
5. Taste and add salt as needed. Add sugar. Serve with a dollop of sour cream on top.

NOTE: Soup will serve about 10. It should not be prepared in batches smaller than this.

## HEARTS OF ROMAINE SALAD WITH BLUE CHEESE DRESSING

Hearts of romaine for 4 to 6

DRESSING:

1/2 lb. blue cheese
1 pint mayonnaise
1 cup sour cream
1½ oz. red wine vinegar
1/2 t. Tabasco sauce
1 t. dry mustard
1/2 clove garlic, crushed

1. Prepare lettuce hearts for serving.
2. Crumble the blue cheese and allow it to come to room temperature.
3. Mix all dressing ingredients thoroughly in a blender.
4. Serve with lettuce hearts.

NOTE:  Place leftover dressing in the refrigerator.  It will keep up to 3 weeks.

***Americans eat better than anyone else in the world—or at least they can.***

## FISHERMAN'S PRAWNS

***This has been one of my favorite recipes for entertaining at home because the preparation is done in advance. Don't marinate too long or the lemon juice will shrivel the prawns. The marinade is really cooking the prawns so broiling them just heats them. Don't broil too long or your prawns will be tough.***

6 prawns per person
Melted butter

### MARINADE

1/2 cup olive oil
3/4 T. salt
3/4 T. oregano leaf
1/2 to 1 clove garlic, finely chopped
1/4 cup horseradish (or less to taste)
1/2 cup dry white wine
1 oz. lemon juice
3/8 cup orange marmalade

1. Shell, clean, devein and butterfly prawns. (Leave tails on.)
2. Combine ingredients and marinate 1 to 2 hours in the refrigerator.
3. Place half of the marinade in a preheated casserole. Arrange prawns in casserole. Drizzle melted butter over the top and broil for 3 to 4 minutes. Serve with buttered rice.

## COEUR À LA CRÈME

***When making the coeur it is important to put the cottage cheese through a fine sieve for smooth texture. Whipping the ingredients makes for a solid mixture. A coeur basket is not absolutely necessary. In fact, at the restaurant we drain the coeur in a colander and then make individual molds.***

1 lb. cottage cheese
1/3 lb. cream cheese
1 t. salt
1/2 T. vanilla
1/4 cup sugar
1 cup whipping cream
Cheesecloth

1. Put cottage cheese through a food mill or a fine sieve.
2. Using an electric beater, mix in cream cheese, salt, vanilla, sugar, and cream. Beat until mixture starts to stiffen.
3. Line a coeur basket with dampened cheesecloth. Pack in the cheese mixture and let it drain for 24 hours in the refrigerator.
4. Unmold on a platter and serve with Strawberry Sauce.

***To cook well you must develop a sense of taste. Cooking is really a matter of balancing flavors.***

## STRAWBERRY SAUCE

10 oz. red currant jelly
1/4 cup sugar
1 oz. brandy
1 T. lemon juice
2 baskets strawberries

1. Mix jelly, sugar, brandy and lemon juice over low heat until liquefied. Chill.
2. Clean and de-hull berries, saving the best to decorate the coeur. Quarter the remaining berries and add to the jelly mixture.
3. Spoon the sauce around the coeur. Decorate with berries and serve.

***There are no secrets to making anything. Know your methods and use good ingredients. When preparing a meal the first thing to remember is to stay sober! Timing is very important. Foods should be ready at the same time. This meal is easy to time since the recipes can be done ahead.***

***I'd recommend that you follow a recipe the first time at home and then make whatever changes you wish. Keep in mind that spices will vary in strength depending on whether they are fresh or dried and that all ingredients will differ from place to place.***

# EL MANSOUR

*Dinner for Four*

*Harira Soup*

*Salade Mohammed V*

*Bastela du Chef*

*Chicken with Lemon*

*Chabackiya*

*Thé à la Menthe*

*Wine:*

*Spanish Red Wine*

*Noppadon Bunnag and Thananone Bunnag, Co-owners*
*Noppadon Bunnag, Head Chef*

El Mansour translates as "The Victor". "In the past six or seven years San Franciscans have discovered Moroccan food," says Thananone Bunnag. He and his brother Noppadon, also the restaurant's head chef, opened El Mansour over two years ago. Both have gained experience over the past nine years by working in various Moroccan restaurants.

"Everything is authentic and traditional here," adds Thananone. "There are no compromises; the food served here is the type found in fine homes and restaurants in Morocco."

Authenticity stretches to decor and eating style. Visitors sit on the floor, use their fingers instead of utensils and wash their hands with towels dipped in rose water. Waiters wear their native costumes.

"Our customers come here for a change. It's exciting to be able to change their habits. We took a lot of chances in the beginning but people like our restaurant."

## HARIRA SOUP

***This is the most popular soup of Morocco.  It will taste even
better if it is prepared a day ahead.***

1 cup lentils
1/2 large onion, finely chopped
1/2 cup parsley, finely chopped
1/4 cup Chinese parsley, finely chopped
1 heaping T. coriander
1 t. black pepper
1 heaping T. ginger
3 T. tomato paste
5 cups lamb stock
Yellow food color (dash)
Salt

1.  Mix all ingredients except tomato paste in a heavy soup pot.  Bring
to a boil and cook for approximately 1½ hours.  Add more water if
mixture becomes too thick.
2.  Add tomato paste.  Correct seasoning.  Serve hot.

### SALADE MOHAMMED V

***It is very important that this salad be well-chilled.***

4 medium tomatoes
1 large bell pepper
1/4 oz. parsley, finely chopped
1½ t. cumin
3/4 t. coriander
3/4 t. black pepper
1½ T. salad oil
2 T. vinegar
3/4 t. salt

1. Place tomatoes in boiling water for about 3 minutes. Peel and chop finely. Drain excess juice.
2. Hold pepper over flame to char the skin. Peel and finely chop.
3. Combine ingredients and correct seasoning.

## BASTELA DU CHEF

***Although the recipe uses 2½ cups chicken, we use a whole bird in the preparation to properly flavor the sauce.***

1/2 onion, chopped
2 T. parsley, finely chopped
1 T. Chinese parsley, finely chopped
1/2 T. ginger
1/2 T. coriander
1/4 T. black pepper
1/2 T. salt
3½ T. salad oil
3 eggs
1 chicken, about 2 pounds
4 cups water
Butter
Powdered sugar
Cinnamon
Filo sheets (available at specialty stores)
Ground almonds (about 2 T.)

1. Preheat oven to 350°.
2. Place chicken, onion, parsley, Chinese parsley, ginger, coriander, salt, pepper, oil and water in a roasting pan. Cook for about 1 hour or until the chicken begins to come away from the bone.
3. Remove chicken from pan. Cool slightly and shred enough to make 2½ cups.
4. Transfer the sauce to a pot and cook for about 30 minutes, stirring often.
5. While heating, add eggs, stirring well.
6. Pass the egg sauce through a sieve. Drain well. Mixture should look dry.
7. Butter a 7 to 8 inch square pan. Lay 3 sheets of filo dough across the bottom, allowing the dough to hang over the edges.
8. Sprinkle almonds, cinnamon and sugar over the dough. Add chicken and cover with more filo sheets.
9. Add egg mixture and fold over the edges of the first 3 sheets. (Part of the egg mixture will be exposed.)
10. Cover with melted butter and place in a hot oven for about 7 to 10 minutes or until brown on top.
11. Flip the bastela upside-down onto a serving dish. Cover top with powdered sugar and cinnamon.
12. Cut into fourths and serve.

### CHICKEN WITH LEMON

***Chicken, lemon, and olives are very common Moroccan foods. In many ways Moroccan food is similar to Algerian cuisine. This recipe represents some of our finer native cooking.***

4 Cornish game hens
2 onions, chopped
1/2 bunch parsley, chopped
1/2 bunch Chinese parsley, chopped
2 T. ginger
1½ T. coriander
1 T. black pepper
1 T. salt
5 T. oil
Water

1. Place all ingredients in a large baking pan. Add enough water to come up about halfway. Place in a 350° oven and cook for about 45 minutes, or until brown.
2. Serve with Lemon Peel (as prepared below).


### LEMON PEEL

4 lemons
4 oz. vinegar
1 T. salt
1 qt. water

1. Score lemons.
2. Combine ingredients and boil for 30 minutes. Discard liquid.
3. To Serve: Peel lemons and evenly distribute peels over birds. Top with chicken cooking juices. For true Moroccan flavor, green olives or slivered almonds which have been browned in butter can accompany the dish.

## CHABACKIYA

1½ cups warm water
1 cup flour
1 T. yeast
Cooking oil
Honey

1. Mix yeast with water. Add flour. Allow to stand for about 20 minutes, uncovered. Mixture will look like thick pancake dough.
2. Heat oil in fry pan to about 300°-330° or hot enough for deep frying.
3. Put pastry dough in a funnel or pastry tube. (If unavailable, make a funnel out of aluminum foil. Make a scoop and cut off the end.)
4. Slowly pour dough into hot oil in one continuous spiral until it is the size of a medium sized cookie.
5. Cook until brown. Turn and brown other side.
6. Remove from oil. Dip into warm honey to cover and serve.

## THÉ À LA MENTHE

***This is *the* drink of Morocco.***

1/2 bunch mint
2 T. gunpowder green tea
Sugar to taste
4 cups water

1. Pour boiling water over mint and tea. Sweeten and serve in glasses.

Note: Do not allow the tea to sit too long or it will become bitter.

# Ristorante Orsi

*Dinner for Six*

*Petrale Sole Meunière*

*Cannelloni*

*Veal Scaloppine Orsi Style*

*Sautéed Spinach*

*Butter Lettuce Salad*

*Chestnuts Flambé*

*Wine:*
*With Sole and Cannelloni—A Dry White Wine*
*With Veal—A Dry White Wine or Light Red Wine*

*Oreste Orsi and Joe Orsini, Owners*
*Oreste Orsi, Head Chef*

"When we opened our restaurant in 1953 we wanted to reflect old San Francisco," says co-owner Joe Orsini. "We chose Florentine decor with San Francisco background.

"Our cuisine is Northern Italian which is very much like French cooking with differences in seasoning. Today you can get the same dish you ordered in 1953 prepared the same way. We do the darndest to be the best at what we know. When you finish here you won't leave hungry or dissatisfied. San Francisco is known for top quality food and that's one tradition we try to carry on."

Co-owner and head chef Oreste Orsi comes from Tuscany where at the age of twelve he began to learn Northern Italian cooking from his grandmother. "She was one of the best cooks, a professional, who was called to France, England and Germany to cook for groups in the times when it took ten days to prepare parties. She taught me the most important part of cooking which is the blending of seasonings." Orsi trained in Florence, Milan and Turin before coming to San Francisco.

## PETRALE SOLE MEUNIÈRE

***Adding half of a lemon to the pan will prevent a heavy fish odor.***

5 oz. filet of Petrale sole per person
Flour
Olive oil
Butter (optional)
Sauterne (dash)
Lemon juice
Parsley

1. Flour fish on both sides. Remove excess flour.
2. Heat olive oil and butter (or olive oil alone) and slowly cook fish.
3. When fish is done, add a dash of sauterne and lemon juice to taste. Serve with parsley.


## CANNELLONI

***Chef Orsi introduced San Franciscans to cannelloni. Prepare the filling ahead of time and let it cool. This will make it more compact and easier to handle.***

3/4 lb. veal, shoulder or loin
1 chicken, about 2½ lbs.
1 lb. ricotta cheese
8 to 10 oz. Parmesan cheese, freshly grated
Nutmeg
6 thin slices Fontina or Monterey Jack cheese
2 cups cream sauce
2 cups tomato sauce
6 pancakes (see below)

1. Cook veal and chicken.  Remove meat from bone and very finely grind.
2. Mix veal and chicken with ricotta cheese and Parmesan cheese.  Add some fresh nutmeg and blend.  Chill.
3. Place some of the mixture in the center of a pancake and roll.
4. Place tomato sauce in the bottom of a baking pan.  Add cream sauce.
5. Add cannelloni and bake in a 350° oven for 10 to 15 minutes.
6. When cannelloni begins to brown, add cheese slices and finish baking.

## PANCAKES

2 eggs
2 T. flour
1 cup half & half
2 T. butter, melted
Butter for cooking

1. Mix eggs, flour and half & half.  Whip until thick and perfectly smooth.
2. Add melted butter.
3. Grease a very hot pan with butter and add about 1 oz. batter.  Swirl to spread evenly and brown.  Turn to brown second side.

NOTE:  Pancakes should be approximately 10 inches in diameter.

## VEAL SCALOPPINE ORSI STYLE

7 oz. veal per person, thinly sliced and pounded
1 lb. mushrooms, sliced
Marsala (dash)
1/2 cup almonds, sliced
Flour
Butter
1 cup sauterne
Parsley

1. Slice almonds and place in the oven to dry.
2. Dredge veal in flour and fry the slices in butter.
3. Meanwhile, sauté mushrooms and add to veal along with almonds.
4. Add wines and cook for 3 minutes. Garnish with parsley and serve.

## SAUTÉED SPINACH

Spinach for 6
Butter
Salt
Freshly ground pepper

1. Wash spinach and blanch.
2. Sauté in butter. Add salt and pepper.

## BUTTER LETTUCE SALAD

***Be sure not to use pasteurized vinegar. Pure wine vinegar is naturally fermented.***

Butter lettuce for 6
Olive oil
Pure wine vinegar
Salt
Pepper

1. Wash and dry lettuce. Tear into pieces.
2. Dress with remaining ingredients.

***Cooking is experience.***

***Food has to be cooked the way *you* like it.***

## CHESTNUTS FLAMBÉ

***The secret of this dessert is a *very hot* chafing dish.  Otherwise, your flambé won't be a success.***

3 lbs. large chestnuts
3 to 4 bay leaves
Fennel seed
Salt
10 T. sugar
14 oz. white wine
Cinnamon (dash)
3 to 4 oz. Triple Sec or Grand Marnier
3 to 4 oz. brandy (100 proof)
Water for boiling

1.  THE DAY BEFORE:  Boil chestnuts with bay leaves, salt and a little bit of fennel seed for about 1½ hours.  Remove from heat and allow to stand, covered, overnight at room temperature.
2.  NEXT DAY:  Remove skins from chestnuts.
3.  Heat the sugar to form a caramel sauce.
4.  Add white wine and cinnamon and boil over low heat for 10 minutes.
5.  Add Triple Sec or Grand Marnier and simmer for just a second.
6.  Place the chestnuts in a chafing dish.  Add the syrup.
7.  Add brandy and flambé.

# L'ORANGERIE

*Dinner for Six*

*Kir*

*Quenelles de Poisson à Notre Manière*

*Carré de Porc à L'Orangerie*

*Pommes Dauphine*

*Money Salad*

*Soufflé aux Framboises*

*Wine:*

*With Quenelles—Robert Mondavi Fumé Blanc
or Meursault St. Anne*

*With Porc—Beaulieu Private Reserve
Cabernet Sauvignon
or Château Mouton-Baron-Philippe, Pauillac*

*With Soufflé—Château Bellevue Contigu-Yquem*

*Roselyne Dupart, Owner*

*Jean-Baptiste Larrateguy, Head Chef*

Oranges were first brought to Europe from the Middle East during the reign of Louis XIV. The French orange grove or l'orangerie soon became fashionable. San Francisco's L'Orangerie opened in 1963 and has won the Holiday Magazine Dining Award every year since 1965.

Maître d'hôtel Hans H. Brandt, who spent twenty years with Trader Vic's and worked at the famous Mural Room at the St. Francis Hotel before joining L'Orangerie, believes that personal service is an essential part of dining. "Food is the foundation of a good meal but no matter how good the food is, if it's not served correctly, something will be missing. A dinner is like the theater or opera; the seating, ambiance and service must all be there to make the evening fascinating. What would Shakespeare be like without good actors?

"We are one of the few restaurants that serve after-theater suppers. Our parties have included Beverly Sills, Leontyne Price, Luciano Pavarotti, Dame Margot Fonteyn and Katherine Hepburn.

"Local clientele is important for a restaurant's color and atmosphere. Our diners feel at home here. Otherwise you have a place where people eat and forget about it."

Head chef Jean-Baptiste Larrateguy, a Basque, came to San Francisco nine years ago. He believes that classes and cookbooks can help the person at home but that the key to preparation is practice.

KIR

***This is a wonderful aperitif!***

Dry white wine such as Muscadet
Crème de Cassis (a few drops)
Twist of lemon

Combine wine with the Crème de Cassis, using enough to produce a light pink color (about 1/2 t. per person). Serve very cold with a twist of lemon.

***The preparation of a fine meal such as this one demands a good deal of time. The fact that the sauces can be prepared ahead of time will help.***

### QUENELLES DE POISSON À NOTRE MANIÈRE

***The hardest thing about making quenelles is producing the proper consistency. The mixture must be firm, yet light.***

1 lb. halibut, boned and skinned
3 egg whites
10 oz. heavy cream
Salt to taste
Nutmeg to taste
Cayenne to taste

1. Pound the halibut and rub through a fine sieve. Place in a sauce-pan and keep cool.
2. Using a wooden spoon, blend the egg whites with the halibut.
3. Gradually add half of the cream, stirring constantly. Add a small amount of each of the seasonings.
4. Place 1/2 t. of the mixture into very hot salted water (not boiling), for 2 minutes to test for consistency and taste. The quenelle is perfect when it has attained the maximum degree of lightness without losing its body. Add more cream and test again, if necessary.
5. Fill a tablespoon with the halibut mixture. Dip another tablespoon in hot water and use it to scoop up the quenelle and invert it onto a buttered sauté pan. Repeat until the whole mixture has been divided.
6. Slowly pour a small amount of boiling water over the quenelles. Season with salt, cover and poach over very low heat for 6 to 8 minutes. Do not boil. Serve with Clam Sauce.

## CLAM SAUCE

***Cook this sauce very gently. It can be prepared two to three days in advance.***

1/2 onion, large, finely chopped
3 stalks celery, finely chopped
1 t. tarragon, finely chopped
15 oz. clams, chopped
8 oz. heavy cream
Salt and pepper to taste
3 oz. butter

1. Melt the butter in a saucepan. Add the onions and cook until they are brown.
2. Add celery, tarragon and clams and cook for 6 minutes.
3. Blend in heavy cream and adjust seasoning. Serve with quenelles.

## CARRÉ DE PORC À L'ORANGERIE

***This is our specialty and has been on our menu since the day we opened. It is something which you can't get in any other restaurant. Boiling the meat removes some of the fat. Remember, though, to boil very gently or the pork will be dry. The sauce can be prepared up to five days in advance and will improve upon standing.***

3/4 of a loin of pork
1½ oranges
Granulated sugar

1. Gently simmer pork in lightly salted water for 1½ hours or until cooked. Remove from water.
2. Arrange skinless orange sections along the top of the pork and sprinkle with sugar.
3. Ladle Sauce à l'Orange over the top and place in a 400° oven for 5 minutes. Serve.

## SAUCE À L'ORANGE

3 oranges
2 lemons
3 T. sugar
3 T. red wine vinegar
1½ cups demi-glace (brown sauce)
1 T. arrowroot

1. Mix the sugar with the vinegar and cook slowly until the sugar has caramelized.
2. Squeeze orange and lemon juice into sugar/vinegar mixture.
3. Blend with the demi-glace.
4. Thicken with arrowroot and continue to heat until the sauce has been reduced (about 3 to 5 minutes).

## POMMES DAUPHINE

19 oz. peeled potatoes

## PÂTE À CHOUX:

3½ oz. hot water
1¾ oz. shortening
2½ oz. flour
3 eggs
Salt (pinch)
White pepper
Nutmeg
Fat for deep frying

1. Cook potatoes as for whipped potatoes. Do not overcook.
2. While potatoes are cooking prepare pâte à choux by combining in a saucepan water, shortening and salt. Bring mixture to a good rolling boil. (Shortening must be melted.)
3. Add flour and cook, stirring with a wooden spoon until mixture is smooth and rolls free from the side of the pan. The mixture should be dry when cooked and not stick to the side. Remove from heat.
4. Add eggs to mixture, blending well after each egg is added.
5. Pass cooked potatoes through a ricer or food mill.
6. Combine potatoes with pâte à choux and season to taste. Blend well.
7. Using a pastry bag and tube form cigar-shaped cylinders of potatoes on a greased paper.
8. Slide potatoes off paper into deep fat (about 350°), and cook until puffed and brown. Drain on absorbent paper and serve immediately.

### MONEY SALAD

***Money salad is the invention of maître d'hôtel Hans H. Brandt. One day a young socialite asked for a good salad which would be light and crunchy. The next day three of her friends came in for the same dish. The first friend mentioned how good it was supposed to be. The second asked what the ingredients were and the third said, 'Well, if X ate it it must be made of chopped money!' The salad should be served with Sauce Vinaigrette.***

4 hearts of artichoke, cooked and very thinly sliced
5 stalks celery, very finely sliced
10 white mushrooms, medium-sized, thinly sliced
2 bunches watercress (leaves only)

1. Take special care to slice the artichokes, celery and mushrooms into almost see-through pieces. Remove the stems from the watercress.
2. Toss lightly with dressing.

### SAUCE VINAIGRETTE

5 oz. olive oil
2 oz. red wine vinegar
1/2 t. Dijon mustard
Salt and pepper (touch)

Mix well and serve with above.

## SOUFFLÉ AUX FRAMBOISES

***This recipe can be prepared ahead of time with the addition of the egg whites just before cooking. The whites must not be under or over-cooked. They should look like snow. Also, they should be carefully added to the other ingredients. There is an old master's secret which advises one to mix in the egg whites with the *left* hand.***

1½ pints fresh raspberries
3 T. butter
3 T. flour
7 oz. scalded milk
5 egg yolks
6 egg whites whipped to soft peaks
4 oz. sugar
3 oz. water
1 large buttered and sugared soufflé dish
Kirsch

1. Melt the butter in a small saucepan. Add the flour and cook slowly for 4 minutes. Cool for a few minutes.
2. Add the milk and cook for 6 minutes. Cool.
3. In another pan combine the sugar and water and cook until boiling. Crush 1/2 pint of raspberries and add.
4. Add the yolks to the cream sauce. In a large bowl combine this sauce with the sugar/fruit mixture.
5. Fold in the whites.
6. Line the soufflé dish with remaining fruit. Sprinkle with sugar and moisten with kirsch.
7. Place the soufflé mixture in the dish and bake at 400° for 12 to 15 minutes.

# El Conquistador

*Dinner for Four*

*Sopa de Albondigas*
*(Meatball Soup)*

*Mexican Salad*

*Tampiqueña Tiras de Filete*
*(Beef Filet, Cheese Enchilada, Refried Beans, Guacamole*
*and Green Chilies)*

*Flan*

*Serve with Mexican Beer such as Carta Blanca*
*or Dos Equis*

*Eddie Armendizo, Owner*

*Alfredo Diaz, Head Chef*

Eddie Armendizo, owner and chef of Grison's Steak House, opened a Spanish-Mexican restaurant, El Conquistador, just a year ago. "Spanish-Mexican food has become popular in the last ten years. I knew Mexican food and wanted a restaurant that would not be typical, where people would enjoy their stay. The decor wouldn't be like others but the restaurant would reflect the same care and quality in food and service that Grison's does. It would be what my regulars have come to expect.

"We decided to take Grison's banquet room and turn it into El Conquistador. At Grison's we do our own meat cutting and use choice eastern beef. The meat, chicken and produce are the same in both restaurants, so we know the quality is the same."

Eddie has been in the business twenty-seven years. "People are eating out more now; they know food and especially wines. You can't fool them. They keep you sharp and on your toes."

Chef Alfredo Diaz is from Durango, Mexico and has been cooking for twenty-two years in Mexico and San Francisco. He was at the Fairmont before joining Grison's.

"Eddie and I talked about a Mexican restaurant and when he called in a decorator, I knew he was serious. I made up the menu, but he had me cook for the staff and get their opinions before the final yes. I've found that a lot of people like hot, spicy food.

"Since I was a kid, I've paid attention to what my mother cooked. I love being a chef and I miss the restaurant on my day off. I like to be here; cooking is fun and a good profession."

## SOPA DE ALBONDIGAS

### MEATBALLS

3/4 lb. ground pork, uncooked
3/4 lb. ground beef, uncooked
1 onion, chopped
1 medium tomato, peeled and chopped
3 cloves garlic
White pepper (dash)
Cumin seed (dash)
1/2 small bunch cilantro
2 eggs
1 T. flour
2 T. rice, uncooked
Salt to taste

### SOUP

1 qt. beef stock (or 1 qt. water plus 1 T. beef base)
2 T. oil
6 green onions, chopped
2 cloves garlic
2 tomatoes, peeled and chopped
1 bell pepper, peeled and chopped

1. Mix meatball ingredients. If a home grinder is used, grind together beef, pork, onion, tomato, garlic and cilantro.
2. Make into small meatballs. Yield will be about 18 to 20.
3. Heat oil and sauté onions and pepper. Add tomatoes and garlic.
4. Add stock (or water and beef base, if necessary) and bring to a boil.
5. Add meatballs and cook 30 to 40 minutes. Serve.

## MEXICAN SALAD

***Keep salad plates in the refrigerator before serving.***

1 head romaine lettuce
1 head iceberg lettuce
12 radishes
1 medium can garbanzo beans
Oil
Vinegar
White pepper
Salt
12 thin onion rings for decoration

1. Slice radishes. Wash and dry lettuce and tear into small pieces.
2. Mix lettuce, radishes and drained beans. Refrigerate to keep crisp.
3. Prepare oil and vinegar dressing. Toss and serve with onion garnish.

***Mexican cooking may seem difficult at first but once you are familiar with the ingredients and methods it will be simple. It is important to follow these recipes exactly to produce the correct flavors.***

## TAMPIQUEÑA TIRAS DE FILETE

I ENCHILADA SAUCE

***This is a true Mexican sauce.***

8 ripe, sweet chilies (4 California chilies and 4 ancho chilies, if possible)
Cumin (pinch)
Oregano (pinch)
Cinnamon (pinch)
1½ oz. Mexican dark chocolate
1 T. sugar
1 T. onion, chopped
2 cloves garlic
Pepper (pinch)
1 bay leaf
Salt
5 T. oil
2 tomatoes
3 qts. water
2 T. flour

1. Place chilies in hot water and let stand 1 hour. Remove from water.
2. Place chilies in a blender together with all other ingredients except oil, flour and onion. Blend and pass through a fine strainer.
3. Heat oil in a saucepan. When hot, add flour and onion and stir about 1 minute. Add sauce and mix well until it comes to a boil. Boil for approximately 10 minutes.

ENCHILADA

14 oz. Monterey Jack cheese, grated
4 tortillas (corn)
Oil

1. Place tortillas, one at a time, in hot oil. Flip to moisten both sides and place on a dish.
2. Put 2½ oz. cheese on each tortilla. Add a small amount of sauce. Roll and cover with sauce and a layer of cheese.
3. Bake in a 450° oven for about 5 minutes.

NOTE: The enchilada sauce can be prepared in advance. In fact, the flavor will improve after 2 days.

II BEEF

2½ lb. filet of beef
4 cloves garlic, crushed
Salt
Pepper
Few drops lemon juice

1. Place filet lengthwise and cutting from top to bottom, divide into 5 oz. portions. Split each portion in thickness and open. (Cut as if splitting a roll.)
2. Add garlic, salt, pepper and lemon juice and let stand 10 to 15 minutes.
3. Cook on a grill or broil. (A charcoal grill is best.)

## III GUACAMOLE

3 avocados
1 tomato
1 diced onion
1/2 lemon
1/2 bunch cilantro
3 green, hot peppers (serrano)
Salt
White pepper

1. Peel avocados and remove seeds.
2. Chop tomato with onion, cilantro and peppers. Make sure mixture
is well blended.
3. Add avocados and mash together. Season to taste.
4. Squeeze lemon juice over top and refrigerate.

## IV REFRIED BEANS

1/2 lb. pinto beans
Salt
1/4 lb. pure lard
2 oz. Monterey Jack cheese, grated

1. Cook beans in water for approximately 2 hours. Drain, mash and
salt to taste.
2. Heat lard in a skillet. Add beans and heat.
3. Add cheese. Heat and serve.

## V GREEN CHILIES SAUTÉ

***We have 10 different types of chilies in Mexico.  Most are hot.***

4 long, sweet, green chilies
1 T. butter
Salt

1.  Place chilies over a flame to char skin.  Peel and cut into strips.
2.  Heat butter in skillet and sauté chilies.  Add salt to taste.

## TO SERVE TAMPIQUEÑA:

Place beef filets and enchilada on each plate.  Place guacamole in center.  Add a small amount of refried beans and green chilies.  Serve with extra corn tortillas and butter.

***Mexican food is flavorful but it need not
be *hot* to be good.***

## FLAN

***This is the most popular Mexican dessert. It can be prepared a day ahead.***

1 cup milk
2 whole eggs plus 2 egg yolks
1 cup sugar
Cinnamon (pinch)
1 t. vanilla

1. Place 1/2 cup sugar in a skillet. Heat to make a caramel sauce, stirring so that sugar doesn't burn.
2. Pour sauce into the bottom of a large or individual serving dish.
3. Combine milk and the rest of the sugar in a mixing bowl.
4. Add whole egg, egg yolks, vanilla and cinnamon. Whip at medium speed for about 10 minutes.
5. Pour mixture into serving dish and place serving dish in a pan filled with enough water to reach halfway. Place in a preheated 350° oven and cook for 40 to 50 minutes, or until set.
6. Refrigerate. Invert to serve.

Scoma's Inc.

*Dinner for Four*

*Calamari Vinaigrette*

*New England Clam Chowder*

*Lazy Man's Cioppino*

*Ice Cream*

*Wine:*

*Charles Krug Chenin Blanc*
*or Wente Brothers Grey Riesling*

*Al Scoma, Owner*

*Efren Navasca, Head Chef*

Scoma's, the famous seafood restaurant, opened twelve years ago on Pier 47. "We didn't know how people would react to a place out of the way," says Al Scoma. "We never dreamed they'd come here and that we would be famous in five or six years. Now we're considered the prime. Celebrities dine here whenever they're in town. We do no advertising yet there are waiting lines every night.

"One night a family had been waiting a long time for dinner and since they were very hungry, I recommended a couple of other restaurants in the area. They left and soon returned saying that since no one was waiting in those places they couldn't have been very good. That was the greatest compliment.

"The hard part of the restaurant business is staying on top. Communication, consistency and common sense are all important. By the way, if you want a good way to know if a restaurant is really tops, take a look at the restrooms."

Head chef Efren Navasca has been cooking for thirteen years, the last ten at Scoma's.

## CALAMARI VINAIGRETTE

***This recipe originated in Palermo and was given to me by a retired San Francisco chef.  The dish can be prepared about twenty to thirty minutes in advance.  Either fresh or fresh frozen squid can be used.***

2 lbs. squid
1/2 medium onion, chopped
2 T. pimento, chopped
2 T. capers
2 T. parsley, chopped
1/8 cup olive oil
1/8 cup wine vinegar
Salt
Pepper

1.  Split squid and remove intestines and gelatinous portions.  Clean well.  Cut into bite-sized pieces.
2.  Parboil squid by bringing water to a boil, adding the squid and cooking for 1 minute, stirring constantly.  Strain and refrigerate.
3.  Mix remaining ingredients and toss with squid.  Add salt to taste and serve.

***Good cooking is a matter of practice.  There are many good cooks who are careless when it comes to fish.  Never use too high a heat . . . and don't overcook!***

***Cooking methods are very important but you must have a talent to be able to really *taste* the food and know if it is too salty or flat.***

### NEW ENGLAND CLAM CHOWDER

***This is our most popular soup. We prepare it daily and I sometimes cook up to eighty gallons per day. This is my original recipe and I recommend that it be served right after cooking for the best flavor. Notice that we use sauterne in this recipe and in our sauces. This is the Italian way and it makes a real difference in flavor. When using frozen clams make certain that they have been frozen no longer than one month or they will have freezer burn. Remember that it is important to mix the flour with the wine before adding it to the soup.***

20 oz. raw clams, chopped
1 pt. half & half
1 cup celery, chopped
1/2 cup white onion, chopped
1/2 cup bell pepper, chopped
1/4 cup flour
2 cups beef stock
1 clove garlic, crushed
1/2 cup sauterne
1 cup potatoes, raw, diced
2 T. olive oil
Salt to taste

1. In a saucepan, brown the garlic in olive oil.
2. Add onions, pepper and celery. Mix in beef stock and bring to a boil.
3. Add clams and potatoes. Cook until potatoes are tender, about 15 minutes.
4. Add half & half and simmer for 5 minutes.
5. Mix flour with wine with a small amount of water. Add the mixture to the simmering soup, stirring well. Cook for another 2 minutes or until it comes to a boil. Salt to taste and serve.

LAZY MAN'S CIOPPINO

***This is a true family recipe developed by Al Scoma's mother in Palermo. Remember to just simmer rather than boil the sauce. If it becomes too thick, add a little more stock or wine. The sugar is added to compensate for the tomato's acidity. The clams do the timing for all the fish. As soon as they open, your cioppino is ready.***

2 28 oz. cans ground tomatoes
1¾ qts. beef stock (fresh or canned)
8 fresh clams
8 prawns, peeled and deveined
6 oz. Bay shrimp
6 oz. crab meat
8 crab legs
1 lb. red snapper, cut into chunks
1 t. oregano
8 bay leaves
1 t. sweet basil
1 T. sugar
Salt to taste
1/4 cup sauterne
1 medium white onion, chopped
1 t. crushed garlic
2 T. olive oil

1.  In a saucepan, brown garlic with olive oil. Add onions and cook until tender.
2.  Add ground tomatoes and beef stock. Bring to a boil and simmer for 30 minutes.
3.  Blend in wine, spices, sugar and salt to taste.
4.  Add seafood. Cook until clams open. Serve with sourdough toast.

NOTE: To cook regular cioppino add 2 whole crabs and reduce the amounts of the other fish.

# Vanessi's

*Dinner for Four*

*Prosciutto and Melon*

*Insalata della Casa*

*Fettuccini al Burro Dolce*

*Veal Piccata*

*Creamed Spinach*

*Zabaione*

*Wine:*

*With Salad — Soave*

*With Fettuccini — Puligny-Montrachet*

*With Veal — Robert Mondavi Gamay*

*Bart Shea and Giovanni Leoni, Owners*

*Giovanni Leoni, Head Chef*

Vanessi's has been called a restaurant that helped to establish San Francisco's reputation as a great eating town.

"We serve basic Italian food with over forty different entrées and four hundred wines to complement the food," says Bart Shea. "Everything, except our roast beef, is cooked to order.

"The restaurant is my greatest enjoyment, it's like my home. I still put in as many hours as I did the first day, twenty-four years ago. The wines are my passion. It's taken twenty years to build that cellar.

"We have a long counter where you can watch the chefs and that counter has taught a lot of women how to cook. They'll order a dish, watch it being done from the beginning, then practice it and come back to find out where they've made a mistake."

Vanessi's has been a long-time favorite with politicians, businessmen and entertainment people. Shea adds, "Over the years I've met many interesting people."

Head chef and partner Leoni learned the art of cooking in Rome and has been with Vanessi's since 1963. "San Francisco is the best town for restaurants," he says. "The people know what they want to eat, and the competition makes you good."

## PROSCIUTTO AND MELON

Cranshaw melon or cantaloupe, **1** wedge per person
Prosciutto, **1** thin slice per person
Lemon slices

On each plate place **1** wedge of melon, **1** slice of prosciutto and a slice
of lemon. Serve.

## INSALATA DELLA CASA

***The oil will get too thick if it is chilled. Add the dressing and toss
just before serving.***

2 heads Belgian endive
2 heads limestone lettuce
1/4 head romaine lettuce

### DRESSING (Per person)

1/2 tomato, very finely chopped
1 green onion, very finely chopped
1/5 clove garlic, cut very finely
1 t. parsley, cut very finely
4 T. olive oil
2 T. vinegar ("Vanessi's brand is very good")
Juice of 1/4 lemon
Salt
Pepper

1. Prepare greens.
2. Mix dressing ingredients and serve with vegetables.

## FETTUCCINI AL BURRO DOLCE

***Use fresh egg noodles if at all possible. It is best to freshly grate your cheese just before cooking.***

2½ oz. noodles per person
1 gallon water
4 oz. sweet butter
5 T. whipping cream
2 egg yolks
5 T. grated Parmesan cheese
1/3 t. freshly ground black pepper (optional)
Salt

1. Cook pasta in salted water for 4 to 10 minutes, depending on particular noodles. They should be cooked al dente. Drain.
2. Return to saucepan and add butter, cream and cheese. Heat.
3. Remove from heat and add egg yolks. Blend well. Add pepper, if desired, and serve.

## VEAL PICCATA

\*\*\*For this recipe have your butcher cut either the top sirloin, top round of the veal leg, or a filet of veal or boneless ribeye. I recommend Provimi veal which is formula raised. Veal should be cooked over a fast fire or it will lose too much of its water content and end up being boiled rather than fried. Also, be sure to use clarified butter whenever braising or sautéeing.\*\*\*

3 slices veal per person (about 1¼ oz. each slice)
4 T. flour
2 t. capers
Juice of 1/2 lemon
4 oz. white wine
3 oz. clarified butter
2 oz. solid butter

1. Pound veal and place in flour. Remove excess flour.
2. Heat clarified butter in a heavy-bottomed aluminum pan. When the butter is almost smoking add the veal. Brown on one side, then turn to brown second. Drain excess fat and arrange veal on a tray.
3. Into the same cooking pan put capers, lemon juice and wine. Reduce to about half the original amount.
4. Add 2 oz. butter, making certain that it is well-blended and melted. Pour sauce over veal and serve.

NOTE: Remember to pound veal to about 1/8 inch thickness or have your butcher do it.

## CREAMED SPINACH

3 bunches spinach
2 T. clarified butter
3 green onions, very finely chopped
4 oz. whipping cream
Salt
Pepper

1. Carefully wash spinach. Cook in salted water and drain.
2. Using a heavy-bottomed aluminum pan, sauté the onions in clarified butter.
3. Add cooked spinach and braise 3 to 4 minutes.
4. Grind or finely chop spinach. Return to pan.
5. Add cream and salt and pepper to taste. Heat and serve.

***A good cook is usually born, not made, but practice helps. The ability to taste is most important. If you don't like food, if you don't like to eat, usually you are not a good cook.***

## ZABAIONE

***The secret of good zabaione is in the whipping. The eggs will scramble if they stay too close to the fire so the whip must reach all of the mixture—sides, bottom, all over. A hand whip is best. The proportion of eggs to wine is important. Since eggs vary in size I suggest using half an eggshell to measure the Marsala and Chablis. This way the proportion will always be right.***

9 egg yolks
9 t. sugar
4 half-eggshells full of Marsala
4 half-eggshells full of Chablis
5 drops fresh lemon juice
5 drops pure vanilla

Using a Pyrex bowl or a copper bowl placed over simmering (not boiling) water, whip all ingredients for 2 to 5 minutes or until mixture is thick. Serve in parfait glasses.

# TRADER VIC'S

*Dinner for Six*

*Peachtree Punch*

*Crab Legs on Ice*

*Bay Shrimp in Chinese Spoons with Wasabi Dressing*

*Fried Won Ton with Sweet and Sour Sauce*

*Bongo Bongo Soup*

*Malay Peanut Chicken*

*Carrots Niu*

*Paké Noodles*

*Chinese Gooseberry Surprise*

*Kafé-La-Té*

*Wine:*
*Sauvignon Blanc or Pinot Chardonnay*

*Victor Bergeron, Owner*
*Tony Paciocco, Head Chef*

Trader Vic's in San Francisco is headquarters for the twenty restaurants in this unique chain and is home for Trader Vic himself, Victor Bergeron.

In 1934, he opened his first restaurant, Hinky Dinks, in Oakland. Four years later, he decided that Hinky Dinks was a junky name. "My wife suggested 'Trader Vic's' because I was always making a trade with someone.

"From the very beginning, it was my philosophy not to serve the same food as our competitors. I knew people wanted different food, interesting food—something they wouldn't cook at home. I call my style of cooking imaginative.

"One of my philosophies in business is to give anyone who comes into my restaurant his money's worth. I want quality. I've never bought a cheap chicken.

"Why the Pacific stuff? It intrigues everyone. You think of beaches and moonlight and pretty girls without any clothes on. It is complete escape and relaxation."

Vic's son Lynn who manages the restaurant adds, "We never scrimp on quality. Everything is fresh. That's important. We cater to very discerning individuals who know good food and enjoy it. Trader Vic's is a very personal restaurant."

For many years Trader Vic has traveled throughout the world collecting recipes, discovering new dishes, and perfecting the exotic drinks for which the restaurants are famous.

## PEACHTREE PUNCH

Per person:

1 peach half (freestone, Del Monte)
1/4 oz. coconut cream
1/4 oz. De Kuyper Peach Liqueur
2 oz. orange juice
1½ oz. Trader Vic's Light Rum
1½ scoops shaved ice
Garnish—skewered peach half, mint, straw, nutmeg

1. Mix ingredients in a blender until peach half is liquefied. Pour into a 17½ oz. stem bowl wine glass and add cube ice to fill.
2. Decorate with skewered peach half across top of glass, mint, a straw and a dust of nutmeg.

## CRAB LEGS ON ICE

Crab legs for 6
Mustard and mayonnaise dressing

Place cold crab legs on a mound of ice. Place dressing in center of ice mound and serve with toothpicks.

## BAY SHRIMP IN CHINESE SPOONS WITH WASABI DRESSING

Bay shrimp for 6

### WASABI DRESSING

1/4 oz. red wine vinegar
1 cup watercress, chopped
3/4 cup sour cream
3/4 cup mayonnaise
1/2 oz. lemon juice
1/2 t. sugar
1/4 teacup wasabi powder (reconstituted)
Salt, pepper, MSG to taste

***Wasabi is a Japanese horseradish which comes in a 4 oz. can in powdered form. To reconstitute wasabi, we simply mix the amount needed with cold water until it becomes a paste. Let the mixture stand 5 to 6 minutes (covered), in order to get the full value of the horseradish.***

1. Combine all dressing ingredients to make a smooth mixture.
2. Serve shrimp in Chinese spoons and top with dressing.

NOTE: Refrigerate the leftover sauce. It will keep up to 1 week.

FRIED WON TON WITH SWEET AND SOUR SAUCE

PORK

1/2 lb. pork
1/4 cup mushrooms
1 T. green onions
Salt and pepper to taste
1 egg yolk
Won ton squares
Peanut oil

1.  Very finely chop pork, mushrooms, and green onions.  Add salt and pepper.
2.  Mix well with egg yolk.
3.  Wrap 1 t. of the pork mixture into a won ton square.
4.  Fry in peanut oil and serve with Sweet and Sour Sauce.

SWEET AND SOUR SAUCE

1/2 cup sugar
1/2 cup distilled vinegar
1/2 cup water
1 T. green pepper, chopped
1 T. pimento, chopped
1 T. mushrooms, chopped
1/2 t. salt
2 t. cornstarch
1 T. cold water

1.  Mix all ingredients except cornstarch.  Boil 5 minutes.
2.  Thicken with cornstarch which has been mixed with water.

BONGO BONGO SOUP

***Follow this recipe exactly for good results. The important thing to remember is that the soup is brought to a simmering point and does *not* boil, otherwise it will turn to paste. If necessary you can use a little chicken stock to thin the soup.***

9½ oz. can oyster purée or equivalent of purée of fresh oysters
1/4 cup spinach, puréed
1 pt. milk
1/4 pt. half & half
1 dash garlic salt
2 T. butter
1 t. A-1 Sauce
2 t. cornstarch
Salt and pepper to taste
Whipped cream (garnish)

1. Heat milk and cream. Add oyster purée, spinach and seasonings and bring to simmering point. Do not let boil.
2. Thicken with cornstarch mixed with a little cold water.
3. To serve top with whipped cream and slip under broiler to glaze to a golden brown.

NOTE: To keep warm place soup in a bain-marie.

## MALAY PEANUT CHICKEN

6 chicken breasts (boneless and skinless)
3 T. Kikkoman Soy Sauce
Salt and pepper to taste
Flour
1½ t. rehydrated onions
6 T. chunky style peanut butter
6 oz. white wine (Wente Dry Semillon)
3 cups chicken stock
6 T. cream sauce
1½ t. red ginger, chopped
1 t. turmeric
2 T. dry golden seedless grapes
1½ cups half & half
2 T. dry roasted peanuts (salted)

1. Season chicken with 1 T. soy sauce. Dust with flour and sauté until golden brown.
2. Add rehydrated onions and wine.
3. Add all other ingredients, except peanuts and half & half, to make the sauce. Simmer for 20 minutes.
4. Remove chicken and place on a serving dish.
5. Finish sauce with half & half. Adjust salt and pepper, if necessary.
6. Pour sauce over chicken breasts and top with peanuts.


NOTE: If recipe is prepared in advance be sure to add the peanuts just before serving.

## CARROTS NIU

1 lb. medium carrots, raw and sliced
2 T. reconstituted dehydrated chopped onions
4 oz. butter
1/2 t. white wine
1/2 teacup chicken stock (plain)
1 t. raw sugar
1 teacup Mendonca's Coconut Milk (milk and solids)
Salt and pepper to taste

1. Sauté reconstituted onions in butter until they are transparent.
2. Add sliced carrots and mix.
3. Pour wine and chicken stock over mixture.
4. Add all other ingredients. Cover and simmer over moderate heat.

***This is the same principal as Carrots Vichy. Try the same with fresh string beans!***

## PAKÉ NOODLES

6 cups noodles, freshly cooked
1 cup plus 2 T. butter
6 T. bread crumbs
2 T. sesame seeds, browned in butter
1 T. MSG
Salt and pepper to taste

Mix the heated noodles with all the ingredients, adding the bread-crumbs last, and serve.

CHINESE GOOSEBERRY SURPRISE

***This is a good seasonal dessert.***

18 Chinese gooseberries (kiwi fruit)
3 oz. raspberry sauce
3 oz. Grand Marnier
Garnish—mint leaves, powdered sugar

1.  Partially cut off the top of the gooseberries. ("Like a cover.")
2.  On each dish place 3 gooseberries in a triangle and put a 1 oz. shot
glass in the middle, filled with a mixture of half raspberry sauce, half
Grand Marnier.
3.  Decorate berries with mint leaves sprinkled with powdered sugar.
Serve.  Use a spoon to scoop out berry and dip into glass or pour mixture into center of berry, then scoop out and eat.


KAFÉ-LA-TÉ

Per person:

4 t. Señor Pico Kafé-La-Té Mix
1 oz. Pisco Brandy
Whipped cream
Hot water

In an Irish mug or ollita combine brandy and Kafé-La-Té mix and fill
with hot water.  Float 1/2 inch of whipped cream on top and serve.

# GAYLORD
## india Restaurant

*Dinner for Four*

*Vegetable Pakoras*

*Chicken Curry*

*Rogan Josh*

*Dal*

*Raita*

*Pilau*

*Gulab Jamun*

*Serve with Beer*

*Kishore Kripalani, President*

*Walayti Ram, Head Chef*

Kishore Kripalani, president of Gaylord, says, "Indian food is becoming very popular all over the world. We are part of an international chain which began in New Delhi in 1941 and which now has thirteen restaurants including New York and Chicago. Gaylord opened in San Francisco in 1976. Each restaurant operates independently.

"Our chefs are from India and are trained by the company to insure the proper preparation of the authentic Northern Indian dishes. Many have been with us over fifteen years. We have specialty chefs for tandoori cooking, for curries, and for desserts."

Diners can see the two tandoors (clay ovens fired with charcoal), which have such intense heat that juices are retained while the meats cook in minutes. "That's why our meats are soft and tender inside.

"The food served here is what you would find in any good restaurant in India," adds Kripalani. "Gaylord has built its reputation on being totally authentic. We never compromise by toning down our food to local taste. A lot of people who love Indian food and know our restaurants expect the same standards in each, so we can't disappoint them."

## VEGETABLE PAKORAS

1 medium potato, finely sliced
3/4 cup garbanzo bean flour
Salt
1/2 t. red pepper
Baking powder (pinch)
Oil for deep-frying
1/4 cup water

1. Mix garbanzo flour, salt, red pepper and baking powder with water to form a fine paste.
2. Dip potato slices in batter and deep-fry over medium heat until cooked.

## CHICKEN CURRY

***The secrets of a good curry are the blending of spices and the order in which the ingredients are cooked. Knowing what proportion of spices to use is an art and comes from the culture and heritage. In India, the individual spices such as cinnamon, cardamom, turmeric, ginger, clove, and so on are mixed in a particular proportion which differs from region to region and family to family. There is no one 'curry powder'. The only way to learn to combine the spices is to start with a minimum amount and then build up. The order of preparation is very important. Most people in America will begin with the meat and then add the spices but this will not produce a true curry. You should begin by frying the onions and some spices until the onions are golden. Add other spices and cook. Now is the time to add the meat or whatever main ingredient you are using. This must brown and then simmer.***

1 chicken, disjointed
2 onions, finely sliced
5 cloves garlic, chopped
2 oz. cottonseed oil
2 cardamoms
2 cloves
Salt to taste
1 small stick cinnamon
1 dessertspoon ground coriander
1/2 t. turmeric
1/2 t. ground ginger
1/2 t. ground cumin
1 t. red pepper
Coriander, finely chopped (garnish)

1. Fry onion, garlic, cloves, cardamoms, and cinnamon in oil until the onions are golden brown.

2. Add other spices and cook over low heat for about 5 minutes, stirring constantly.

3. Add the chicken and cook on a slow fire for a few minutes or long enough to give the chicken a light brown color.

4. Add enough water to form a thick gravy. Cover the pot and simmer the chicken until tender.

5. Garnish with finely chopped coriander and serve hot.

ROGAN JOSH

***Most of Indian food is pot-cooking. This and tandoori baking are our basic processes. For each dish there is a change in the spices.***

1 lb. lamb
6 oz. onions
6 cloves garlic, ground
Salt to taste
1/2 cup yoghurt
4 oz. vegetable oil
1 oz. ground coriander
1 t. red pepper
1/2 t. curry powder
1 small piece ginger
1 t. Garam Masala (see recipe below)
Green coriander leaves (garnish)

1. Marinate the lamb with 2 oz. of ground onions, coriander and yoghurt.
2. Heat the oil and fry the remaining onions with ground ginger and garlic until the onions are golden brown.
3. Add the remaining spices and the marinated lamb and cook for 5 minutes or until the lamb takes on a brown coloring.
4. Add water to form a thick gravy and cook until the lamb is tender.
5. Sprinkle Garam Masala onto mixture and serve garnished with green coriander leaves.

### GARAM MASALA

6 cloves
6 peppercorns
6 cardamoms
1 t. cumin seeds
2 small sticks cinnamon

Carefully blend all ingredients.


### DAL

***Dal and raita are standard dishes served with curry. In many ways Indian food is like Chinese cuisine in that four or five dishes are shared for one meal.***

1/2 lb. yellow lentils
2 oz. butter
1/2 t. red pepper
1/4 t. turmeric
1/2 t. cumin seeds
2 cloves garlic
1 small piece of ginger, finely sliced
1 medium onion, finely chopped
1 tomato, chopped
Salt to taste
Fresh coriander, chopped (garnish)

1. Boil the lentils with half of the onion and the turmeric, garlic, ginger, and salt.
2. In a separate pan, fry the rest of the onion in butter until it is light brown.
3. Add red pepper, cumin seeds and tomato.
4. Immediately mix the boiled lentils with the mixture and garnish with chopped coriander.

## RAITA

***In India many families may not eat meat. In order to maintain a balanced diet a meal will include lentils, grain and yoghurt.***

1/4 cucumber
1 tomato
4 spring onions
1 lb. unflavored yoghurt
Salt to taste
Red pepper (pinch)
Mint (optional)

1. Skin and chop the tomato and the onions. Grate the cucumber.
2. Mix all the ingredients and serve cold.

## PILAU

***At Gaylord's we bake our bread every day.  For this dinner, however, the rice takes the place of bread.***

1 cup rice
2 onions, finely chopped
6 cardamoms
4 peppercorns
2 T. butter
6 cloves
Salt to taste
2½ cups water

1.  Wash the rice thoroughly.
2.  Heat the butter in a deep pot and fry the onions.  Add the rice and crushed spices.
3.  Add water and salt and boil until the water evaporates.

NOTE:  Keep the pot in a hot oven for a few minutes to dry the extra water left behind in the rice.

## GULAB JAMUN

\*\*\*Indian desserts are complex and demand a good deal of attention.
This is one of our less complicated ones and should not be too hard
to prepare at home.\*\*\*

1 lb. milk powder (whole cream)
1/2 lb. sweet butter
2 lb. sugar
Oil to fry

1. Mix the milk powder and butter to a fine paste.  Form into 24 balls.
2. Deep fry the balls over a very slow fire to give them a golden brown
color.
3. Make a sugar syrup and soak the balls in the syrup for 5 to 7 minutes or longer, and serve.

NOTE:  The sugar acts as a preservative so the balls can be prepared
the night before.

# Le Club

*Dinner for Six*

*Prawns Sauté*

*Salad Matrimonial*

*Saddle of Lamb and Chestnut Purée*

*Raspberry Soufflé*


*Wine:*
*With Prawns — Beaulieu Vineyard Chablis*
*With Lamb — Robert Mondavi Pinot Noir*
*With Soufflé — Château d'Ay Champagne, 1970*


*John Parsons and J. Edward Fleishell, Owners*
*Guy Grenier, Head Chef*

Before it was Le Club, this intimate restaurant was a private club for the people who lived in the exclusive Clay-Jones apartment building. In 1969 it was bought by J. Edward Fleishell and John Parsons. They have kept the original flavor and continue to pamper their clientele which is 90% San Franciscan.

Maître d'hôtel Brian Griffin, with the restaurant since the beginning, has worked with the Cunard Lines and at the Four Seasons in New York. He first came to San Francisco on vacation and never left. Griffin says, "We do our own thing and don't copy anybody. We buy the best and never cut corners. There are a lot of gourmets in this world and since dining out is expensive, it is important to give them their money's worth. If you're not happy with a dish here, let us know by sending it back. The problem can be rectified right away."

Chef Grenier started cooking at fifteen and later worked at Chamonix. He was at La Caravelle in New York before joining Le Club nine years ago.

## PRAWNS SAUTÉ

***It is best to use fresh prawns. If they are not available use fresh frozen which have been frozen for just a short time. Defrost in the refrigerator. Also, be sure not to overcook. These take just two to three minutes.***

18 prawns
1 glass dry white wine
Ginger
Salt
Pepper
Juice of 1 lemon
Butter
8 oz. lobster bisque soup
2 T. cream
Parsley, chopped

1. Marinate prawns in a mixture of wine, ginger, salt, pepper, and lemon juice for 6 hours.
2. Sauté in butter.
3. Add lobster bisque and cream. Mix well, heat and serve with chopped parsley.

## SALAD MATRIMONIAL

***Remember to toss just before serving.***

1/2 lb. Belgian endive
1 bunch watercress
3 heads limestone lettuce
Oil
Vinegar
Salt
Pepper
French mustard (about 1 t.)

1. Prepare greens.
2. Make dressing by mixing oil and vinegar in a 3:1 proportion. Add salt, pepper and mustard to taste.

## SADDLE OF LAMB AND CHESTNUT PURÉE

\*\*\*Ask your butcher to bone the saddle. Keep the bone to place under the meat while roasting. This will make a better juice and will prevent burning. Lamb should not be served too rare or it will be gristly. Most Americans tend to overcook. Lamb is at its finest when it is served medium pink. At Le Club we tell the degree of doneness by pressing the meat with a finger. If the meat is soft and responds to the touch, it is rare. If it is hard and does not respond, it is well-done.\*\*\*

6 lb. saddle of lamb
8 oz. white wine
Thyme (pinch)
2 cloves garlic
Salt
Pepper
Cornstarch
4 fresh artichoke bottoms, cooked
Chestnut purée (canned)
Butter
Sugar

1. Place bone under meat and roast at 450° for 15 minutes.
2. After 15 minutes, remove the saddle and de-glaze with the wine, thyme, garlic, salt and pepper.
3. Add cornstarch, as necessary, to thicken.
4. Season chestnut purée with butter and sugar to taste.
5. Stuff artichoke bottoms with purée.
6. Serve meat with sauce and stuffed artichoke bottoms.

NOTE: Be sure to remove the saddle from the refrigerator and bring it to room temperature before cooking. Serve with pommes soufflé or suitable potatoes and fresh vegetables.

# RASPBERRY SOUFFLÉ

***This can be prepared two to three hours ahead and kept in the re-
frigerator before cooking. Place in the oven about twenty minutes
before serving.***

8 oz. puréed raspberries
Sugar to taste
6 oz. flour
6 egg yolks
1 jigger raspberry brandy
10 egg whites
2 oz. sugar
Sweet butter

1. Place puréed raspberries in a saucepan and bring to a boil. Add
sugar to taste.
2. While raspberries are boiling, make a mixture of flour and egg yolks.
Blend thoroughly and add to raspberries. Mix again.
3. Bring to a boil and then cook, stirring occasionally to prevent a
skin from forming.
4. When dough is firm, add brandy and mix.
5. Beat egg whites until firm, adding sugar. Fold into dough until well
blended.
6. Coat a soufflé dish with sweet butter and sugar. Make sure that dish
is well covered with both. Add batter and bake at 380° for about 20 to
25 minutes.

***You can cook anything but the only way to learn is by doing. Like
everything else, cooking is trial and error. Don't cut corners; buy the
best that's available.***

# PAPRIKÁS FONO

*Dinner for Six*

*Veal Paprikás*
*(Borju Paprikás)*

*Galuska*

*Cucumber Salad*
*(Uborka Saláta)*

*Paulette's Torta*
*(Walnut Roulade filled with Bittersweet Chocolate Cream)*

*Wine:*

*With Veal, Galuska and Cucumber Salad—*
*Debröi Hárslevelü*
*(A Dry White Wine from the Northern Slopes of Hungary)*

*With Torta—Tokaji Aszu "4 Puttonyos"*
*(From the Tokay Region—Known as the "Nectar of the Gods")*

*Paulette and Laszlo Fono, Owners*

Hungarians Laszlo and Paulette Fono believe that dining must be a total experience and that their restaurant Paprikás Fono should be a true introduction to Hungarian cuisine. Everything from food to decor is authentic and the meals served are described by Mrs. Fono as "those cooked in family kitchens in the different regions of Hungary".

Laszlo Fono, a former Olympic skier, admits that operating a restaurant can be very much like preparing for a sports event. "You must be in condition," he says. Fono's first restaurant, The Magic Pan, which introduced his crêpe pan, opened thirteen years ago and is greatly responsible for the present popularity of crêpes in America.

The menu at Paprikás Fono reflects the owners' personal tastes. While planning the restaurant Laszlo Fono would often prepare his favorite food for friends. "I could see in their eyes that they liked it," he says. "If they did, I trusted that others would as well."

Paulette adds, "Our restaurant appeals to all types of people. This is our home and we believe that if you give people good food and hospitality, they will be appreciated."

## VEAL PAPRIKÁS

***Paprika has a very exciting history. Columbus first brought it to Europe from the New World and the Turks brought it to Hungary in the 16th century. Hungarian peasants used paprika as a medicine. Actually, it is the most nutritious of all seasonings and is the richest food source of Vitamin C.

Paprika, of course, is an essential part of Hungarian cuisine. There are many different types, each differing in sweetness, color and heat. Here at our restaurant, we use 200 or more pounds per month, primarily in our gulyás (goulash), and in our veal, chicken and mushroom paprikás. This is one spice which should be used by the tablespoon, not the pinch. Paprika is not just for color but for taste! When cooking, keep in mind that the paprika must be properly dissolved and that it burns easily.

In Hungary they say that if you eat lots of paprika you get rosy cheeks, you have lots of energy and you have a healthy life.***

Veal leg, about 3 lbs.
2 to 3 medium onions
3 T. paprika
1 green pepper
1½ cups water plus 1 T. water
2 t. salt
1/2 t. white pepper
1 rounded T. flour
1/2 cup sour cream
5 T. cooking oil

1. Cut veal into 1 inch cubes. Dice onions into fine cubes.
2. In a 4 to 5 quart heavy casserole or Dutch oven, sauté onions in oil over low heat for 5 minutes, or until golden. Stir frequently.
3. Remove casserole from heat. Add paprika and mix well.
4. Place cubed veal on top of paprika mixture and turn pieces to coat them well. Brown over low heat for a few minutes, stirring constantly. *Make sure that paprika does not burn.*

5. Gradually add green pepper, 1½ cups of the water, salt and white pepper. Cook over low heat for about 40 minutes. Taste for seasoning and remove green pepper, discarding it. Test veal for tenderness, being careful not to overcook or the meat will fall apart.

6. In a bowl, mix flour and sour cream with remaining 1 T. cold water. Add 4 T. warm paprika sauce from cooked meat to sour cream and blend well making sure that there are no lumps. Add sour cream to sauce in pot and mix well. Serve at once or reheat over low heat before serving.

NOTE: If you are preparing the recipe the day ahead do not add sour cream until the day it is served. Noodles or rice may be substituted for galuska.


## GALUSKA

***The American public is accustomed to pasta but often finds it difficult or time consuming to make. The 'galuska' or 'light egg dumpling', is not difficult to prepare. We especially recommend a gadget known as a galuska maker which is available in most cooking supply shops.***

3 cups flour
2 T. salt
3 eggs
1 cup water
1 T. cooking oil
4 T. butter
Water for cooking

1. Mix flour and 1 T. of the salt in a large mixing bowl.
2. Add eggs and water. Using a wooden spoon, beat about 2 minutes until evenly blended and no large lumps of egg and flour remain.
3. Scrape dough from sides of bowl. Pour oil on top of dough to prevent drying, but do not mix into dough.

4.  Meanwhile, melt butter, preferably in the bottom of an ovenproof serving dish.

5.  In a large pot, bring 3 quarts of water to a boil.  Add remaining 1 T. salt.

6.  Use a spaetzle maker to form 1/2 inch square pieces from the dough. (Dough will be gooey and thin.)  Or, spread one-third of the dough along the edge of a cutting board and cut strips about 6 inches X 1/2 inch. Cut each strip into 1/2 inch squares.  (Dip knife in hot water to make clean cuts in dough.)

7.  Quickly drop the squares into boiling water as you cut them. After a rapid boil the galuska will float to the top of the water when done.

8.  Strain and briefly rinse with cold water, if desired.  Repeat entire process until all the dough is used.  Place in the serving dish in which the butter has been melted.  Serve immediately or store, covered, in the refrigerator and reheat later.

NOTE:  You may wish to cook the dough in portions as it takes only 1 to 3 minutes to cook.  If the water begins to boil over while cooking, stir it with a wooden spoon.  The heat can be turned down as long as the water continues to boil.

TO REHEAT:

Place galuska in an ovenproof serving dish and cover with foil.  Punch holes in foil to release steam.  Heat at 350° for 10 to 15 minutes or cook on top of stove in a double boiler for 10 to 15 minutes, making sure to keep the water in the lower pot boiling throughout cooking time.

## CUCUMBER SALAD

\*\*\*This is one of our most popular salads and it features our special sweet and sour dressing. In Hungary, it is customary to serve the salad with the main course.\*\*\*

3 to 4 cucumbers
1¼ cups water
1 T. salt
1/4 cup sugar
1/3 cup white vinegar
1 or 2 cloves garlic, mashed
Sour cream
Paprika

1. Peel cucumbers using a potato peeler. Remove only the skin, not the flesh. Thinly slice.
2. In a mixing bowl, combine water and salt.
3. In a separate bowl, combine sugar, vinegar and garlic. Pour vinegar mixture into salted water and stir well.
4. Strain and pour dressing over sliced cucumbers. Let stand in a cold place at least 1 hour before serving. Garnish with sour cream and paprika.

NOTE: Do not use a wooden bowl.

## PAULETTE'S TORTA

***Desserts are very popular in Hungary. This torte is one which I
learned to make by watching my mother at home. We have a saying,
"Why use flour when you can use nuts?" After all, nuts are very good
for you. And remember to save the trimmed cake and eat it fresh.
It's delicious!***

## TORTA

8 eggs, separated
8 T. sugar
6 T. ground or grated walnuts
2 T. flour
Butter
Grated chocolate
Torta Cream (see below)

1. In a large bowl, beat egg yolks and sugar for 2 to 5 minutes or until
the mixture is pale yellow, creamy, and forms a ribbon as you beat it.
2. Mix together walnuts and flour. Add mixture to egg yolks, mixing
well. Do not mix too long or batter will get stiff.
3. In a separate bowl, beat egg whites until shiny and stiff peaks form.
Add 1/3 of egg white foam to batter. Use a spatula to fold in whites
gently but well.( This will lighten the texture of the batter and make it
easy to fold in the rest of the egg whites.)
4. Gently fold in remaining egg white foam with the spatula, turning
in one direction only.
5. Butter a 10 X 16 X 2 inch baking sheet or a 9 X 14 X 2 inch cake
pan and dust with flour. Spread batter evenly in pan.
6. Bake at 350° for 35 to 40 minutes or until cake tests done.
7. When cake is done, gently invert on clean towel and roll up jelly roll
fashion. Cool completely before spreading on cream.

### TORTA CREAM

1 t. decaffeinated coffee powder (or instant coffee)
1/3 cup fresh coffee
1 cup sugar
1/4 cup milk
8 T. unsweetened cocoa
3 sticks (1½ cups) unsalted butter, room temperature

1. In a small saucepan, dissolve coffee powder in hot, fresh coffee. Add sugar. Cook over medium heat until sugar is totally dissolved and mixture has boiled slightly.
2. Reduce heat so mixture is no longer boiling. Add milk. (Do not boil or mixture will separate.)
3. Strain cocoa to remove lumps and stir it into the coffee mixture, slowly beating to a smooth paste. Let cool 10 minutes.
4. Add butter and beat until smooth and creamy. Cover and refrigerate 45 minutes to 1 hour until cream is thick and spreadable but not too hard. Stir occasionally while in refrigerator because outer edges of cream will chill faster than middle.

## TO PREPARE ROLL:

1. Cut a piece of waxed paper a little longer than unrolled cake. Lay unrolled cake on paper.
2. Trim 1/4 inch from all sides of cake.
3. Evenly spread two-thirds of cream on cake, then roll up gently. using waxed paper to help in the process.
4. Spread remaining cream over top and sides of roll. Sprinkle top with grated chocolate. Refrigerate.


NOTE: "You can substitute fruit preserves for the chocolate cream. Apricot or raspberry are best. Spread preserves on unrolled cake just as you would the chocolate cream. A thin layer of whipped cream can top the preserves, if desired. Roll up and sprinkle top and sides of cake with powdered sugar. Top with slices of fresh fruit for garnish. Also, unsweetened carob powder may be substituted for the cocoa in the original recipe." (Torta will yield 12 to 14 slices.)


***Jo étvágyat kivánok! (Bon appétit!)***

## APPETIZERS

| | |
|---|---|
| Avocado à la Horcher's (Ernie's) | 29 |
| Bastela du Chef (El Mansour) | 93 |
| Bay Shrimp in Chinese Spoons (Trader Vic's) | 142 |
| Calamari Vinaigrette (Scoma's) | 127 |
| Cannelloni (Ristorante Orsi) | 99 |
| Crab Legs on Ice (Trader Vic's) | 141 |
| Fettuccini al Burro Dolce (Vanessi's) | 134 |
| Fried Won Ton (Trader Vic's) | 143 |
| Little Snails in Clay Pots (Fournou's Ovens) | 11 |
| Marinated Prawns (Mama's) | 67 |
| Petrale Sole Meunière (Ristorante Orsi) | 99 |
| Prawns Sauté (Le Club) | 161 |
| Prosciutto and Melon (Vanessi's) | 133 |
| Quenelles de Poisson à Notre Manière (L'Orangerie) | 108 |
| Sashimi (Yamato) | 49 |
| Tortellini (Ernie's) | 29 |
| Tortellini Vincent Price (Mama's) | 68 |
| Vegetable Pakoras (Gaylord India Restaurant) | 151 |
| Vitello Tonnato (The Blue Fox) | 41 |
| Vol-au-Vent of Crab Legs and Lobster Amoricaine (Doros) | 3 |

## BEVERAGES

| | |
|---|---|
| Café Amaretto (Mama's) | 71 |
| Kafé-La-Té (Trader Vic's) | 147 |
| Kir (L'Orangerie) | 107 |
| Peachtree Punch (Trader Vic's) | 141 |
| Thé à la Menthe (El Mansour) | 95 |

## DESSERTS

| | |
|---|---|
| Chabackiya (El Mansour) | 95 |
| Chestnuts Flambé (Ristorante Orsi) | 103 |
| Chinese Gooseberry Surprise (Trader Vic's) | 147 |
| Coeur à la Crème (The Golden Eagle) | 86 |
| Dacquoise (Fournou's Ovens) | 16 |

## DRESSINGS, SAUCES AND SPECIAL SEASONINGS

# ENTRÉES

| | |
|---|---|
| Abalone Speciale de la Casa (Mama's) | 69 |
| Beef Sukiyaki (Yamato) | 53 |
| Beggar's Chicken (The Mandarin) | 59 |
| Boneless Loin of Lamb, Verdi (The Blue Fox) | 44 |
| Button Mushrooms and Lobster (Kan's) | 23 |
| Carré de Porc à L'Orangerie (L'Orangerie) | 110 |
| Chicken Curry (Gaylord India Restaurant) | 151 |
| Chicken with Lemon (El Mansour) | 94 |
| Chicken Livers Sauté (The Mandarin) | 58 |
| Clams Elizabeth (Sam's Grill) | 77 |
| Eggplant and Pork Szechwan Style (The Mandarin) | 61 |
| Fisherman's Prawns (The Golden Eagle) | 86 |
| Lazy Man's Cioppino (Scoma's) | 129 |
| Malay Peanut Chicken (Trader Vic's) | 145 |
| Oyster Beef (Kan's) | 24 |
| Roast Native Duckling (Fournou's Ovens) | 12 |
| Rogan Josh (Gaylord India Restaurant) | 153 |
| Saddle of Lamb (Le Club) | 162 |
| Sai Wo Duck (Kan's) | 21 |
| Schroeder's Sauerbraten (Schroeder's) | 35 |
| Sesame Chicken (Yamato) | 52 |
| Tampiqueña Tiras de Filete (El Conquistador) | 119 |
| Tempura (Yamato) | 50 |
| Tournedo de Boeuf Rossini (Ernie's) | 30 |
| Veal Paprikás (Paprikás Fono) | 167 |
| Veal Piccata (Vanessi's) | 135 |
| Veal Scaloppine à la Doros (Doros) | 5 |
| Veal Scaloppine Orsi Style (Ristorante Orsi) | 101 |

# SALADS

| | |
|---|---|
| Belgian Endive and Watercress Salad (The Blue Fox) | 43 |
| Butter Lettuce Ravigote Salad (Fournou's Ovens) | 15 |
| Butter Lettuce Salad (Ristorante Orsi) | 102 |
| Caesar Salad (Doros) | 4 |
| Cucumber Salad (Paprikás Fono) | 170 |
| Guacamole (El Conquistador) | 121 |
| Hearts of Romaine Salad (The Golden Eagle) | 84 |

## SOUPS

## VEGETABLES, RICE AND NOODLES

# NOTES

# DINING IN—THE GREAT CITIES
### A Collection of Gourmet Recipes from the Finest Chefs in the Country

_____ Dining In—Baltimore
_____ Dining In—Boston
_____ Dining In—Chicago
_____ Dining In—Dallas
_____ Dining In—Denver
_____ Dining In—Hawaii
_____ Dining In—Houston, Vol. I
_____ Dining In—Houston, Vol. II
_____ Dining In—Kansas City
_____ Dining In—Los Angeles
_____ Dining In—Minneapolis/St. Paul
_____ Dining In—Monterey Peninsula

_____ Dining In—Pittsburgh
_____ Dining In—Portland
_____ Dining In—St. Louis
_____ Dining In—San Francisco
_____ Dining In—Seattle, Vol. II
_____ Dining In—Toronto
_____ Dining In—Vancouver, B.C.

_____ Feasting In—Atlanta
_____ Feasting In—New Orleans

*Forthcoming:*

_____ Dining In—Manhattan
_____ Dining In—Philadelphia

_____ Dining In—Sun Valley
_____ Dining In—Washington, D.C.

☐ CHECK HERE IF YOU WOULD LIKE TO HAVE A
DIFFERENT **DINING IN**— COOKBOOK SENT TO YOU
ONCE A MONTH

Payable by Mastercard, Visa or C.O.D. Returnable if not satisfied.
*$7.95 plus $1.00 postage and handling for each book.*

BILL TO:
Name _____
Address _____
City _____ State _____ Zip _____

☐ Payment enclosed      ☐ Send COD

☐ Charge

Visa # _____
Exp. Date _____
Mastercard # _____
Exp. Date _____

☆ Signature _____

SHIP TO:
Name _____
Address _____
City _____ State _____ Zip _____

- - - - - - - - - - - - - - - - - -

Name _____
Address _____
City _____ State _____ Zip _____

- - - - - - - - - - - - - - - - - -

Name _____
Address _____
City _____ State _____ Zip _____

**PEANUT BUTTER PUBLISHING**
PEANUT BUTTER TOWERS • 2733 - 4TH AVENUE SOUTH • SEATTLE, WA 98134